THE ACTIVIST WPA

THE ACTIVIST WPA

*Changing Stories about Writing
and Writers*

LINDA ADLER-KASSNER

UTAH STATE UNIVERSITY PRESS
Logan, Utah
2008

Utah State University Press
Logan, Utah 84322–7800
© 2008 Utah State University Press

Manufactured in the United States of America
Cover design by Barbara Yale-Read

ISBN: 978-0-87421-699-8 (paper)
ISBN: 978-0-87421-700-1 (e-book)

Library of Congress Cataloging-in-Publication Data

Adler-Kassner, Linda.
  The activist WPA : changing stories about writing and writers / Linda Adler-Kassner.
    p. cm.
  Includes bibliographical references.
  ISBN 978-0-87421-699-8 (pbk. : alk. paper)
  1. English language–Rhetoric–Study and teaching–United States. 2. Report writing–
Study and teaching (Higher)–
United States. 3. Writing centers–Administration. I. Council of Writing Program
Administrators (U.S.) II. Title.
  PE1405.U6A325 2008
  808'.042071073–dc22
                              2007051418

CONTENTS

PREFACE AND ACKNOWLEDGMENTS

In the yoga class that I took each week while I was writing this book, our teacher, Michael, reminded us to practice *pranayama*, breath that vibrates in the back of the throat. (Michael described it as the breath you make if you're trying to fog up a mirror.) "Hearing everyone else's breath," he said, "reminds us that we practice in a community—we don't practice alone." Instead, we're a group. If we need help with poses we can look around us at fellow practitioners to see what they're doing. It also reminds us to focus on the here and now—to be in *this* moment, in this time and space. Not two minutes ago, not in the future—now, now, and now. Together, here, now.

Together, here, and now are three ideas that run throughout this book. When I described this project to people who asked about it (and even those who didn't), I would tell them that I was working on a book about strategies for writing program administrators (WPAs) and writing instructors to employ to affect policy. But this shorthand summary doesn't really do justice to the work involved in "developing strategies," or to the ways of thinking and working that emerged during the process of research, thinking, and writing this book. Instead this is really about understanding ourselves as WPAs and teachers and working from this understanding to enter into relationships that invariably continually change that understanding in sometimes unexpected and surprising ways. Our breath is our own, yes. But when we hear the breath of others and develop our practice in concert with others, that practice changes in ways we don't always anticipate. The work that has gone into this book has changed my own practice as a teacher and administrator— even a person outside of the world of work—in ways I never could have anticipated. It's given me invaluable gifts—time, ideas, insight, humor, wisdom, reflection—and I have greedily accepted them, turning them over and around to think about how I can incorporate them into my own practices.

• • •

Whenever I pick up a new (academic) book, I look at the acknowledgement page to see who shared in the experience of the authors in the creation of the work. I'm painfully aware of the conventions of acknowledgment-as-genre; in this instance, as in those others, the thanks I convey here go far beyond the words that appear on this page. I literally couldn't have written this book without the groups and individuals I list here (and a lot of others I don't because of space constraints).

When I started to think about how to undertake the research for this book, I realized quickly that I wanted to learn from others who had experience learning about organizational cultures and developing strategies within those cultures. I of course looked to academic sources; however, I also wanted to spend time with others who were engaged in this kind of work with real people. For this, I turned first to my friend Gary Magenta, vice president of sales and marketing at Root Learning, a strategic engagement company. Gary made it possible for me to attend presentations, talk with Root staff, and get a broad sense of Root's methodology for learning about client cultures. Katie Outcault, Root's director of strategic innovation and client services, was also incredibly generous with her time, allowing me to participate in team meetings and to talk with her team about how Root gathers and uses information.

This book would not have been possible without the community organizers and media activists who generously shared their ideas, their time, and their incredible wisdom with me: Eleanor Milroy of the Industrial Areas Foundation; Erik Peterson from Wellstone Action; Bruce Budner from the Rockridge Institute; Anat Shenker-Osorio from Real Reason; Normon Solomon; Laura Sapanora from the SPIN Project; Michel Gelobter from Redefining Progress; and Joan Blades from MoveOn.org and

Moms Rising. Additionally, during the time I spent with Anat, she brought me to a presentation by Alan Jenkins of the Opportunity Agenda (OA). While I did not spend the same kind of one-on-one time with him that I did with others listed here, I have benefited from him and OA's work as well. Each of these organizations is working to change stories about *their* issues in innovative, challenging, and *successful* ways—and we can continue to learn from them all (I've included contact information for each organization in the appendix). I am also grateful to the NCTE staff who took time to talk with me about their work to change stories about writers and writing: Kent Williamson, Ann Ruggles Gere, Paul Bodmer, Barbara Cambridge, and Millie Davis.

Second are the people who helped me think about and work through the connection between spirituality, especially Jewish spirituality, and the ideas here. I benefited enormously from an early and formative conversation with Rabbi Robert Levy of Ann Arbor's Temple Beth Emeth (TBE), who generously shared his time to listen to the ideas of a neophyte Jewish philosopher. Jan Price of the Ann Arbor Jewish Cultural Society, my own community of practice, both listened to my ideas and shared her amazing talent, knowledge, and wealth of resources with me as I worked through early ideas about Judaism included here. Aimee Rozum provided both insight and support as I worked through the process of writing this book. I also am grateful to TBE's Cantor Annie Rose and participants in the Jewish spirituality seminar that Annie led in late 2006. The members of this group formed a community where I, a non-TBE member, felt safe and comfortable raising hard questions about the ways that I (and others) enact our beliefs and principles. I am also grateful to my colleague Jeff Bernstein, a colleague from Eastern Michigan University's political science department for his input on chapter 6.

My friends in our fantastic profession of composition and rhetoric, as always, provided enormous support during the process of writing and revising this book. Dawn Skorczewski read most of this book and provided both helpful comments and great cheerleading along the way. My friend and EMU colleague

Cathy Fleischer also read much of this work in progress, providing incredibly amazing and speedy feedback in the clutch. Heidi Estrem, Susanmarie Harrington, and Sherry Linkon have read many pieces of this manuscript in various forms, also sharing advice, reassurance, and chocolate along the way. I met Shawn Hellman at the 2007 WPA conference; she volunteered to read a revision of chapters 1 and 6 and also provided remarkably thorough and insightful comments. Eli Goldblatt is a great model of what it looks like to be an "academic" who is involved in the community. My colleagues in the Council of Writing Program Administrators Network for Media Action (WPA-NMA)—especially Dominic Delli Carpini, Darsie Bowden, and Pete Vandenberg—have made thinking about all of these ideas fun, interesting, and as collaborative as can be. I'm also grateful to WPA-NMA members for sharing vignettes about their WPA experiences with me for chapters 4 and 5 of this book. As successive presidents of the Council of Writing Program Administrators, Chris Anson and Shirley Rose have both supported and encouraged the WPA-NMA's work. This book has its origins in a conversation that Chris, Shirley, and I had one night during the 2004 National Council of Teachers of English (NCTE) conference about the challenges that writing instructors and WPAs faced; the next morning, running through the dark streets of Indianapolis, I sketched the outline for it in my head. At the Conference on College Composition and Communication (CCCC) the next year, when I had a firmer sense of the project, I sought out Michael Spooner to see if Utah State University Press might be interested in the manuscript. Michael's encouragement has been unwavering from that time on. Michael and Utah State have been a joy to work with from start to finish.

I am also thankful for the incredible group of colleagues I now have at Eastern Michigan University. I've already mentioned Cathy Fleischer; Heidi Estrem (now at Boise State, but always with us in spirit) and Carol Schlagheck read and provided great advice on portions of this book. As department head, Russ Larson provided enormous support for EMU's First Year Writing

Program. Ann Blakeslee, Steve Krause, Cheryl Cassidy, Doug Baker, and Steve Benninghoff all listened to and supported me through the process of writing this book, as did two remarkable former EMU graduate students/instructors, Jennifer Castillo and Liane Robertson. My thanks also to Alicia Vonderharr, who indexed it for me.These colleagues make it challenging (in the good sense) and fun to come to work every day. EMU also supported this work with a research leave for the 2006–07 school year, and I am thankful to the Josephine Nevins Keal Fund for a grant to support the travel required for this book.

Acknowledgments sections always mention the author's family, but in this case this book was a real family affair. My husband Scott Kassner provided incredible moral support, reminding me that I *could* write this book and (as is typically the case) being far more patient with me than I am with myself. A Renaissance kind of guy, Scott read and provided incredibly helpful feedback on the sections of this book that deal with historical narrative *and* provided flexibility with family time, especially during the time I spent on the road for research. Our daughter, Nora Kassner, knows more about most things than we do; she also indulged me in conversations about teaching, learning, administration, and organizing work as I've put this book together. My brother, Bill Meyer, put me up (and put up with me) for eight days of research work in San Francisco and put me in contact with Norman Solomon while busily teaching his own history classes at Marin Academy and preparing for the academy's annual Conference on Democracy. Finally, I would be remiss if I didn't thank my original organizing teacher, my mother Connie Adler. Now retired from her career as a professional activist, editor, and all-around hell-raiser, she is busily taking photographs, acting as the secretary of the bio-diesel co-op, hiking around with the dogs, traveling, fulfilling responsibilities in the native plant co-op, sitting on the board of a new charter school, and joining "the progressive community" (her words) for coffee every Saturday morning at ten o'clock in Silver City, New Mexico. She provides an incredible model for activists everywhere.

THE ACTIVIST WPA

interested in changing the stories about writing; writers; quality; etc.

1

WORKING FROM A POINT OF PRINCIPLE

STORIES TOLD ABOUT SCHOOL: WRITERS AND WRITING

Alarmist stories about student writers or college-level writing that run counter to the ones that circulate among writing teachers on disciplinary listservs or in discussions in professional research are easy to find. Using the search terms "writing skills and college students" in a database like Lexis Nexis Academic reveals news items headed by such titles as "Grammar Is Making a Comeback; Poor Writing Skills Among Teens and a New Section of SAT Fuel Return to Language Basics" (DeVise 2006) and "Students Fall Short on 'Information Literacy,' Educational Testing Service's Study Finds" (Foster 2006). Ask people on the street about student writing, and one typically hears a dazzling array of stories attesting to problems with (college) students' writing as well.

What don't come up as often in news media or in conversation are stories suggesting something else—that everyone can write; that students are astoundingly knowledgeable about composing in contexts that some teachers know relatively little about; that schools are being put in virtually untenable situations with regard to literacy instruction; or that it might be worth questioning the criteria by which "quality" is being determined. That's because these stories do not fall within the rather tight frame currently surrounding discussions of education more generally. Instead, typical are stories like those that follow the headlines above, or one from the December 3, 2006, suburban *Chicago Daily Herald* that begins, "The majority of freshmen attending area community colleges left high school unprepared to take college-level classes, statistics from local community colleges show." The next paragraph continues: "More than half of recent high school graduates attending these two-year colleges required remedial help—in courses that don't count toward a degree—because they lacked fundamental skills in math, reading, or writing" (Krone 2006).

For as long as I have taught composition—going on 20 years—I have listened to some people outside of the field (faculty colleagues, professionals outside of the field, people I meet on airplanes, administrators on the campuses where I have worked) tell stories like the one in the *Chicago Daily Herald*. Students can't write; they read the wrong things or not at all; they aren't prepared or they have to take "remedial" courses; teachers (college, high school, middle school, grade school, presumably preschool) aren't teaching them "what they need to know." I would venture to guess that nearly anyone teaching writing (or English) has heard this lament. These claims form the core of a story about writers and writing classes that seem to resonate particularly strongly now.

I have also long thought about how to tell other tales about students, writing, and the work of teaching writing. This desire to work from different stories—in fact to change the dominant story about the work of writing instruction—comes out of my own experience as a student, a person living and working in the community, and as a composition instructor and program administrator. As a field, composition and rhetoric seems to be turning its attention to thinking strategically about how to shape stories about students and writing. As I listened to and talked with colleagues about going about this work I realized that it might be useful—certainly for me, but perhaps for others as well—to think about it as systematically and strategically as we do, say, the research that we conduct or the courses that we design. To pursue this interest, I've immersed myself in textual research about how we might go about this work of telling other stories, and I've spent time with and listened to community organizers and media activists who engage in this work on a daily basis. The result is this book, *The Activist WPA: Changing Stories about Writing and Writers.*

The key word here is *story*. Robert Coles, the psychiatrist and student of documentary production, provides an especially useful way to think about stories. Coles explains that as a child, he found the stories that his parents read to him helped them put his experiences in a broader perspective. When Coles began to think about relationships, for example, his mother suggested he read *War and Peace.* In college, Coles took a course with noted literary scholar Perry Miller; reading William Carlos Williams's poetry during that course, he decided to contact the physician and poet. Williams invited Coles to shadow him as he worked with patients in Patterson, New Jersey. Following Williams and hearing his stories, Coles implies, led him to choose a career in medicine rather then teaching English. Coles goes on, in the early stages of *The Call of Stories,* to describe other *personal* stories that shaped his experiences as a professional.

Coles' discussion of his own stories telescopes out from *personal significance* to broader, *social* significance. During psychiatric training, for instance, Coles heard patients differently if he asked them for and listened to *their* stories. They became not lists of symptoms to be addressed or behaviors to be modified, but whole people whose existences were comprised of these tales. As a result, Coles became interested in "the many stories we have and the different ways we can find to give those stories expression" (Coles 1989, 15). Coles also realized that he understood patients' experiences through his own, that his personal story extended to the ways in which he used others' stories to construct a broader experience. And studying school desegregation in the south during the early 1960s, he realized that the ways in which these stories were constructed had consequences far beyond himself or his patients. Coles writes that:

> [The children whom he was observing in southern schools] were going through an enormous ordeal—mobs, threats, ostracism—and I wanted to know how they managed emotionally. It did not take me long to examine their psychological "defenses." It also did not take me long to see how hard it was for many of those children

to spend time with me. . . . I attributed their reserve to social and racial factors—to the inevitable barriers that would set a white Yankee physician apart from black children and (mostly) working-class white children who lived deep in the segregationist Dixie of the early 1960s. That explanation was not incorrect, but perhaps it was irrelevant. Those Southern children were in trouble, but they were not patients in search of a doctor; rather, their pain was part of a nation's historical crisis, in which they had become combatants. Maybe a talk or two with me might turn out to be beneficial. But the issue for me was not only whether a doctor trained in pediatrics and child psychiatry might help a child going through a great deal of social and racial stress, but what the nature of my attention ought to be. (25)

The power of this portion of Coles's book, which for me culminates in this excerpt, is the ways in which he moves between explanations of the power of personally grounded stories for individuals (himself, his patients) and the ways in which those stories, when seen as a collective body, testified and gave witness to a larger one that had gone relatively unexplored.

Using the concept of framing—that is, the idea that stories are always set within and reinforce particular boundaries (described more thoroughly later in this chapter)—it is possible both to examine how the same telescoping phenomenon of storytelling is occurring around writers and writing instruction today. That is, there are *different* stories circulating about writing and writers that build cumulatively to form larger narratives, all with "messages omitted, yarns gone untold, details brushed aside altogether . . . " (Coles 1989, 21). In this book, I am especially concerned with the stories that are perpetuated through news items like the ones quoted at the beginning of this chapter, because I do not believe that they reflect what we know, as a field, about writers' abilities or about the best ways to help students develop their writing abilities. However, the concept of framing also is useful for considering strategies to create other kinds of stories. This book, then, addresses these three issues: examining some of the stories currently surrounding writing

instruction (chapters 1, 2, and 3); considering what frame sur-
rounds those stories (chapters 2 and 3); and considering how
we might use strategies developed by community organizers and
media strategists to shift those frames (chapters 4 and 5). This
chapter introduces this work by discussing concepts of stories,
frame, and ideals and strategies.

IDEALS WITH STRATEGIES

The "arguments" in this book, such as they are, are closely
related to a quote (from Karl Llewellyn, the leading "legal
realist" of the twentieth century) that I'll invoke throughout:
"Strategies without ideals is a menace, but ideals without strategies is a mess [*sic*]." I discovered this mantra on the back chalk-
board in a classroom at the University of Michigan Law School
where I was attending a talk by Bill Lofy, author of a biography
of Paul Wellstone. Wellstone, a two-term Democratic Farmer-
Labor (DFL) senator from Minnesota from 1990–2002, was
killed in a plane crash during the 2002 campaign season. As a
former Minnesotan, I had volunteered for several of Wellstone's
campaigns and knew that I wanted to use Wellstone Action, the
organization founded after his death, as a research site for this
project because of the smart and successful ways that the organization was training activists and political candidates around the
country. But while Wellstone Action is now well-known for this
kind of strategy training, when Wellstone himself arrived in the
Senate he positively oozed ideals, but he sorely lacked strategy.
Lofy (and others) point to many moments where Wellstone
was abrupt with or alienated Republican congressional leaders
(and members of the executive branch) to illustrate this lack
of "strategic" thinking. But as Wellstone developed into a smart
and savvy politician, he developed strategies that enabled him
to make alliances across the aisle and, as a result, to both take
principled stands and achieve bipartisan support for his goals.

The first argument here extends from the second part of the
Llewellyn quote. If we take Wellstone's experiences as a model,
WPAs and writing instructors have been all over the map: filled

with ideals but without any kind of core or shared strategies. In her 1986 study of writing programs, Carol Hartzog noted that she did not find "any unanimity about the form and ultimate value of work in this field" (1986, 68). She went on to ask a question about how to connect ideals (such as belief in the value of writing for "critical inquiry" at the core of "academic processes and structures") with strategies: "Who holds and can exercise authority in this field" (69)? The power, she explained, "still resides in English—and other—departments. . . . As long as there is uncertainty about what composition is, the question of what place it holds on campus—and in the academy—will remain central" (70). Without a clear sense of institutional or disciplinary identity, the implication here is that writing programs have no clear base from which to work strategically. Instead, writing "disappear[s]"—"it absorbs the strategies, wisdom, and language of other departments, and it serves them in turn" (70).

What Hartzog identified as a vexing issue related to positioning becomes, 16 years later, a sense of frustration for Peggy O'Neill, Ellen Schendel, and Brian Huot. Writing about what they saw as a need for WPAs to acknowledge "writing assessment [as] a form of social action," they noted, for example, that missing from discussions of assessment (e.g., on the WPA-L listserv) was an understanding of assessment (as a strategy) that must be situated in the complex contexts of our field and our institutions. "Although we may help each other satisfying our immediate needs in responding to calls for help [when providing information about systems and/or prompts that "work," for instance]" they write, "we are also promoting an uncomplicated, practical approach to the assessment of writing that cannot only belie the complexity of assessment but also make ourselves, our programs, and our field vulnerable to the whims of administrators and politics because issue of power, values, and knowledge-making converge on assessment sites, with very real consequences to all stakeholders" (O'Neill, Schendel, and Huot 2002, 13). This sense of disconnection between strategy and ideals can still be heard regularly on the WPA list when, for instance, subscribers send (regular and necessary) pleas for fast solutions to immediate problems.

At the same time, there is a growing body of WPA research that attests to WPAs' desires to blend ideals and strategies, to engage in WPA work as strategic action. In his preface to Joseph Janangelo and Kristine Hansen's *Resituating Writing*, Charles Schuster (quoting Susan McLeod) identified WPAs as "change agents," stressing "the importance of WPAs possessing the vision, knowledge, and ethos to alter institutional philosophies and practices" (Schuster 1995, x). Other essays in that collection address questions of how to balance ideals and strategies in WPA work, from the construction of writing programs (Janangelo) to the role of computers in composition instruction (Romano and Faigley 1995) to writing across the curriculum (WAC) work (McLeod 1995). Two specific areas of WPA research, especially, have provoked the subfield toward more focused attention on the balance between strategies and ideals: assessment and labor issues. This is perhaps because both deal explicitly with questions of ethics, specifically the treatment of human beings. A few examples of scholarship focusing on each subject illustrate the ways that authors have blended strategies and ideals as they address these questions. Kristine Hansen asks, "How can [the WPA] in good conscience lead a program that is built on exploitation" (24)? Eileen Schell argues that "as we hasten to professionalize writing instruction and make broad claims for its importance as a democratizing force, we must make parallel efforts to address one of the most pressing political problems in composition studies. . . . the gendered politics of contingent labor" (Schell 4). In what are less response-focused pieces, essays in the co-edited *Tenured Bosses and Disposable Teachers* assert and address a pointed argument leveled in Marc Bosquet's essay: "The lower-managerial lifeway of fighting for personal 'control' [by the WPA] over instructional 'resources' [including program instructors] and disciplinary status recognition is very different from the ethos of struggle usually associated with social and workplace transformation:

the raising of consciousness, the formation of solidarities, coalition building, and so on" (Bosquet 2004, 15). Joseph Harris
has called for a "new class consciousness" in composition that is
rooted in shared commitment: to first of all address to improve
working conditions for instructors (including part-time and
graduate instructors); to have instructors at all ranks teach first-
year writing; and to improve the working conditions of instructors, including the salaries and benefits that they receive (Harris
2000, 58–64).

Assessment researchers like O'Neill, Schendel, and Huot,
have challenged WPAs and writing instructors to use notions of
validity developed by assessment researcher Pamela Moss and
others that necessarily engage questions of ideals (goals, aims,
ultimate objectives—as well as whose interests are represented
in those ends) and strategies (the means by which those objectives are measured and achieved). As Peggy O'Neill explains,

> Validity research involves a dynamic process that requires an exami-
> nation of procedures and results, use of this information to revise
> and improve assessment practices, and an examination of revised
> practices in a never-ending feedback loop. In short, validity inquiry
> should be embedded in the process itself, ongoing and useful,
> responsive to local needs, contexts or changes, something that is
> never really completed. (2003, 51)

Brian Huot's *(Re)Articulating Writing Assessment* develops this
conception of validity in even greater detail. Huot argues that
"including theoretical input about the complexity and context
necessary to adequately represent written communication as
part of the validity process gives writing teachers and writing
program administrators a real say about not only the ways
in which student writing is assessed, but also in the ways it is
defined and valued" (Huot 2002, 52). This conception of validity is also represented in the notions of "meaningfulness" and
"ethics" that Patricia Lynne places at the center of assessment
work. She writes that

"meaningfulness" draws attention specifically to the purposes for and substance of any given assessment practice. Meaningful assessment, then, should be conducted for specific and articulated reasons, and its content should be intelligible to those affected by the procedure. 'Ethics' draws attention to assessment as it is practiced and specifically to the relationships among those involved in the process. (Lynne 2004, 15)

It is also embedded in Bob Broad's notion of dynamic criteria mapping, a process that, Broad argues, allows for examination of the intersections between writing and both local (classroom, programmatic, institutional) and disciplinary contexts (Broad 2003, 119–120).

The argument here and in all these examples repeats an implicit or explicit case that I see in this text that echoes Llewellyn's quote. There are clearly WPAs and writing instructors who are interested in telling stories about writing instruction and writers that represent our values and ideals—who want, in fact, to construct narratives that are akin to historiographer Hayden White's conception of tropes, "movement[s] *from* one notion of the way things are related *to* another notion, and a connection between things so that they can be expressed in a language that takes account of the possibility of their being expressed otherwise" (White 1978, 2). But to engage in this process of story construction or story changing we must also constantly find what Darsie Bowden called this "chi," (Bowden 2007) this balance between *ideals* and *strategies*.

STORY MAKING

The first part of *The Activist WPA* addresses this concept of identifying ideals. Ideals are our personal stories and motivating factors—the things most important to us. They extend from what we hold in ourselves, what we see through our emotions and experiences, what Coles calls "compelling part[s] of our psychological and ideological makeup" (Coles 1989, 24). Whatever strategic work we do must take these into account and extend from them, in much the same way that Coles's story of his own experiences telescopes from the individual to the more social and general. In other words, the strategies that we use and the stories that we tell ourselves and others about why those strategies (and their hoped-for outcomes) are important are rooted in other stories, ones that we tell about *why* we do the work that we do and motivate us to persist in it. In this chapter I'll refer to these things primarily as "principles," a term also used by Nell Noddings (2005), but others have used different terms to refer to them: "core principles" (Elbow 2000d); "foundations" (Miller and Santos 2005). As I'll discuss below, these principles extend from "lived experience" (Ronald and Roskelley) and sometimes require us to undertake the potentially uncomfortable process of self-examination.

In this chapter, I'll describe stories from my own experience that I find motivational and which have propelled me to the work that I do. These stories both reflect and have led me to two important principles which I will also discuss in the concluding chapter: the concept of *tikkun olam*, which stems from my (cultural) practice as a Jew, and the idea of prophetic pragmatism which is rooted in my experience as a teacher and a researcher. In addition to serving as a personally important theory, pragmatism has also provided a number of foundational principles for American approaches to education. But because of the particular nature of pragmatism and the stories which underscore it, the principles embedded in pragmatism have become available to individuals and groups holding very different perspectives regarding the purposes of education—that is, the *ideals* that education should strive to achieve—and the *strategies* through which they should be accomplished. Educators—compositionists and/or WPAs—who want to change stories must understand this historical back story, lest we invoke versions of it that ultimately undermine the very points that we are trying to advance. This back story, the narrative emanating from the progressive pragmatic jeremiad and its relevance for education, is the subject of chapter 2. Chapter 3 then examines how, in contemporary education, this narrative has also become the backbone for stories about education that ultimately undermine the authority of teachers. Following this analysis, chapters 4 and 5 borrow from work developed by community organizers and media strategists to offer potentially useful strategies for WPAs and writing instructors to construct connected, historically mindful, stories about writing and writers on their campuses and, perhaps, beyond. Chapter 6, finally, returns to the exigencies facing WPAs and writing instructors in these complicated times and raises a call to action.

FRAMING

The beginning of this chapter draws on a number of news items that reflect (and tell) a story about writing or, in White's terms, repeat a trope. As I indicated, I have worked in my career to tell other stories (as have many others in the field); I have also experienced frustration that I think is shared by other WPAs and writing instructors regarding the difficulty of changing that dominant narrative. (When I was drafting this chapter, in fact, there was a discussion on the Conference on Basic Writing Listserv [CBW-L] about a relatively recent report condemning student writing and the work of writing instruction, making the case that "postmodern theorists" have led to a shift in composition courses away from "traditional" instruction and toward something else. As one respondent said [in a post typical of the discussion], "this small minded and dishonest 'analysis' of what happens in writing classrooms—and what applications of theory to pedagogy actually mean—gets my blood boiling" [Lalicker 2007]). My own frustration indicates a difference in the frames surrounding stories about writing and writers—one that is dominant (and used to frame stories like the ones cited above), and others that are less often featured.

Framing is a concept initially advanced by sociologist Erwin Goffman, who suggested that frames helped individuals "rely on expectations to make sense of everyday experiences" (Reese 7). Early conceptions of framing drew on the culturally oriented critique of Antonio Gramsci's conception of "commonsense," especially as was elaborated by Raymond Williams, to suggest that frames define stories that both reflect and perpetuate dominant cultural values and interests rather than "stimulating the development of alternative conceptions and values" that are "critical" of those values and interests (Deacon et al. 1999, 153). According to communication theorist Stephen Reese,

> Framing is concerned with the way interests, communicators, sources, and culture combine to yield coherent ways of understand the world, which are developed using all of the available verbal and visual symbolic resources. . . . Frames are organizing principles that are socially shared and persistent over time, that work symbolically to meaningfully structure the social world. (Reese 11)

Frames extend from symbols—words, phrases—to signifiers. The more often the signifiers are invoked in association with the word (by producers, consumers, and interactions between them), the tighter the association between symbol and signified, and the less likely that the signifier (around the word, image, or subject matter) will permit "alternative" interpretations. Communication scholars James Hertog and Douglas McLeod refer to the symbols at the core of the frame as "code words," words that trigger "excess meanings" that are included in (and therefore reinforce and strengthen) existing stories already extending from the code word. In Hertog and McLeod's conceptualization, a frame might look like a concept map. At the center of the frame is a symbol (a word, a phrase) that is tightly linked to closely related issues that emanate from and refer back to the frame. From each issue are links that extend from (and refer back to) the central node in the frame; extending from those are other issues, and so on. The farther from the central node issues become, the more closely they are linked to other issues and other nodes; thus, they "act as bridges" to those other nodes (Hertog and McLeod 2001, 140). Issues and nodes are triggered through the use of words or structures which, in turn, are linked to narratives and myths. Activating a narrative will in turn trigger connections to others, and the "meaning" comes from the "pattern of relations" among the nodes and issues (140).

Most of the code words included in the first two paragraphs of the news item from the *Chicago Daily Herald* cited at the beginning of this chapter—"underprepared," "remedial help," "count toward a degree," and "fundamental skills"—are linked to a story that says, "The educational system is failing in its mission to prepare students for higher education. As a result, colleges are being forced to offer courses that are neither real college courses, nor deserving of real college credit. Because students are lacking skills when they arrive, instructors are being required to waste their time—and taxpayer dollars—on providing these courses." Another code word, "statistics," is used to signal that the research supporting this narrative is absolutely true and unbiased.

But WPAs and writing instructors might interpret this story—and these code words—quite differently. (In fact, the CBW-L post from Bill Lalicker, quoted above, signals his different interpretation of the report to which he is referring; the authoring body sees it as legitimate, while he sees it as "small minded and dishonest.") Drawing on best practices, position statements from National Council of Teachers of English (NCTE) or from the Council of Writing Program Administrators (WPA), or from research in composition and basic writing, an alternative narrative might say: "Definitions of 'good writing' are context dependent. What is seen as 'good writing' in one context might not be seen as such in another (e.g., Bartholomae 1985; Royster; Bawarshi 2003). That's why, in composition classes, we should focus on what students can do when they arrive, rather than working from what a potentially arbitrary placement exam says they cannot do, then build on that knowledge and help students develop strategies to analyze and meet new expectations (e.g., WPA 2007; NCTE 2004; Haswell 1988; Royer and Gilles 1998; Huot 2002). Students bring a wide array of literacy skills to college (e.g., NCTE 2004; Gee 1996; Chiseri-Strater 1991); in writing classes they can identify how to use those skills and develop new ones. All college classes are worthy of college credit if they are asking students to do challenging, college-level work" (e.g., Adams 1993; Fox 1999; Grego and Thompson 1996).

Consider the range of other issues (in the field) that are related to the code words in this story. They include placement (How are students are placed in writing courses? Through what measures? Why? What is the criteria by which their literacies are measured?); course and program assessment (How are grades in writing courses determined? Why? How are courses within a program achieving the outcomes set for the program? What are the criteria for assessment? How are they determined? Why?); hiring (Who should teach writing courses? How should they be trained? Compensated? Why?); and course and program structure (Who should support the work of the writing course/program? Why?). In fact, using the concept mapping strategy, it is possible to construct a map from this story that would extend to three central questions encompassing nearly every question or issue addressed in the field's professional literature:

- How should students' literacies be defined when they come into composition classes?

- What literacies should composition classes develop, how, and for what purpose?

- How should the development of students' literacies be assessed at the end of these classes?

From here, it is possible to draw speedy connections to other issues that are nearly ubiquitous in discussions among WPAs and writing instructors: How should students be assessed when they come into college? By whom? Through what measures? What should the curriculum of composition classes be? Who should teach them? What should we do with nonstandardized forms of language in the writing class? What is the best way to foster students' development as writers? (Brian Huot would likely make the case that these—and all else in composition—boil down to questions about assessment, which I think is also accurate [Huot 4–7].)

One need look no farther than some of the resources in the field to establish the dominance of these issues. CompFAQ, for

instance, is a Web site started by Richard Haswell and Glenn
Blalock in response to the kinds of frequently posted questions
to the WPA listserv mentioned earlier, those pleas for fast solutions to vexing questions. But rather than provide responses
situated only in local contexts, it attempts to provide a space
where respondents can build evidence around disciplinary
consensus by compiling composition research that is "in such
general agreement that one would think that it would constitute
a point of received general knowledge in the field of comp,
like the principle of DNA in biology" (Williams 2005). Some of
the issues included there include responses to questions like:
"What is the content of composition courses?" "How are writing
programs being assessed?" "What is the empirical evidence demonstrating that Comp 101 is working?" "What are the minimum
competencies students need to be prepared for/successful in
[the first semester course]?" NCTE's Web site, similarly, has
over 100 position statements that reflect best practices in the
fields of English language arts and composition and rhetoric;
among them are statements on class size, writing (and reading)
instruction, timed writing, the ACT and SAT writing exams, and
other issues that affect the working lives of writing instructors
and WPAs on a daily basis. These questions come up repeatedly
because they are central to what it is that writing programs *do*.
The ways they are framed—in both question and response—
shape every aspect of our working lives. If we want to have a
voice in the discussion about those lives, then we need to think
about frames and the stories that emerge from them.

WPAs and writing instructors are hardly alone in objecting
to the ways that writing instruction is discussed in mainstream
media—our K-12 colleagues(in a variety of fields) are way ahead
of us. Susan Ohanian, Denny Taylor, Nell Noddings, Alfie Kohn,
and Herb Kohl are but a few of the luminaries who have written
loudly and long about the ways that control over education—
including control over the way that education is framed—have
been systematically taken away from teachers. A hypothetical
frame that Nell Noddings includes in her book *The Challenge to*

Care in Schools illustrates the degree to which "what is possible" has been constricted:

> If we suppose that we know exactly what schools should accomplish, we can analyze more effectively the current debate over accountability in higher education. However, advocates of accountability may disagree substantially on what it is that schools should accomplish. . . . Many critics object to the narrow emphasis on test scores, and a few even suggest that schools should now be held accountable for widespread fear among students, a possible drop in graduation rates, the demoralization of teachers, and the growing corruption of administrators who are using questionable strategies to keep schools off the failing list. It does seem reasonable to hold schools responsible for the direct effects of enacted policies, whether those effects are intended or not. (Noddings 2005, xvi)

Just as questioning the meanings associated with code words like "underprepared" or "remedial" in the Chicago Daily Herald story might seem preposterous to the everyday reader, so the idea of holding schools accountable for dropping graduation rates, teacher morale, and administrator corruption also might seem unreasonable or unrealistic. But testing for these factors is in fact just as "real" an option as assessing students' "achievement" on standardized assessments—it's just that the frame that has been constructed around these assessments makes this alternative possibility seem silly or uncommonsensical.

Whether or not there is some degree of consensus regarding the three questions linked to the code words and issues that extend from stories about student writing and writers inside of the field of composition and rhetoric is an intriguing question, though it is not one I will dwell on here. As I'll discuss in chapters 4 and 5, this is because one of the central tenets of the strategies for story-changing here is that it is most effectively accomplished at the local level, and the strategies described in chapters 4 and 5 offer several possibilities for how to develop and cultivate consensus among campus and community colleagues.

To be sure, it is useful—and important—to martial the support of "national" voices in this work, especially when we are trying to establish a basis for it that extends beyond our programs or campuses. But there *are* position statements, "best practices," and research journals circulating in the field that reflect our field's best attempt at consensus positions on issues. As I mentioned above, the NCTE (at 60,000 members) has developed an array of position statements on issues ranging from class size to reading pedagogy; the process used by the NCTE for this work, from identifying topics to crafting a final statement, has brought in the voices of members from a wide range of institutions. WPA (at 500 members) has developed a set of outcomes for first-year composition that serves as the basis for over 250 writing programs; the WPA also has official statements on the intellectual work of WPAs, on plagiarism, and a range of position statements for members through its Network for Media Action. The collective research and teaching experiences represented in these documents are vast, and can be understood to represent a consensus around some of the most vexing issues facing WPAs and writing instructors.

THE STEADY SOUND OF DRUMBEATS

But despite efforts to advocate for the positions in (and frames surrounding) these professional documents and statements, Joseph Harris notes that we have not been particularly effective at affecting discussions about that work beyond the field. "Ask anyone *outside* the field (and this includes many writing instructors who are not active in CCCC) what they expect students to learn in a composition course," Harris laments,

> and you are likely to hear a good bit about issues of proper form and correctness. . . . What I find . . . distressing has been the ongoing inability of compositionists (including myself) to explain ourselves to [people outside the profession]. Instead we have too often retreated behind the walls of our professional consensus, admonishing not only our students and university colleagues but the more

general public when they fail to defer to our views on language and learning. (1997, 85–86)

The problem, as Harris explains it, is with framing the stories that are told about the work of writing instruction. More precisely, there are "frame conflicts" (Ryan 1991) around those three key issues that I've identified above: what students bring to college writing classes (how their knowledge should be assessed and valued); what they should learn in those classes (from curriculum to pedagogical style); and how their learning should be assessed (and, prior to assessment, defined and conceptualized). That is, these issues are framed differently by those inside the field than by those outside of it. These issues, as I suggest above, extend out to include virtually all of the work of writing instructors and WPAs. The stories (or narratives) that circulate among writing instructors and WPAs about these issues often emanate from different interpretations, different frames, than those circulating outside of the field.

Furthermore—and probably more importantly—these stories have consequences. They encompass every aspect of our work, from placement to curriculum design to classroom instruction to professional development. While we may not yet be feeling the full force of these consequences in college composition work, we need look no further than to our colleagues in K-12 instruction to find out what happens when others control the frame that determines, at least in part, how classroom work is carried out. I refer here in part to No Child Left Behind (NCLB) and to Reading First, an Education Department program that, according to the Department's Reading First Request For Proposals, "focuses on putting proven methods of early reading instruction in the classroom" (http://www.ed.gov/programs/readingfirst/index.html). Reading First has forced schools—particularly elementary schools—to virtually abandon whole language reading instruction. Consider Bess Altwerger's essay, "Reading for Profit: A Corporate Coup in Context":

Many of us have witnessed this cataclysmic change in education with both shock and awe—shock that we could have returned to a bygone pretheoretical era in reading instruction when children "read" meaningless texts and teachers taught letters and sounds with manual in hand; awe at the sources of power and influence that so swiftly and stealthily stole our nation's schools and classrooms from us, their rightful guardians: teachers, parents, and communities. We stand in near paralysis as our school systems continue to loot our reading programs and curricula by order of state and federal law and then punish and demean us when their own mandates don't meet their expectations for success. (2005a, 2)

As a result of NCLB penalties and Reading First restrictions, says Altwerger, "teachers are 'trained' to follow the scripts and directions in the teachers manuals [of commercial reading programs] as if they are unskilled workers. States are refused federal dollars when they stray from official prescribed components of reading instruction and assessment, and they must resort to hiring federally "approved" consultants [who often work for, or conduct research by, the companies producing the programs] to right their paths" (Altwerger 2005a, 3).

The endemic corruption of Reading First has been documented as thoroughly and rigorously as the "theory in practice" foundation Altwerger refers to. In 1998, Denny Taylor's *Beginning to Read and the Spin Doctors of Science* documented the corrupt processes through which direct instruction programs like Open Court (published by McGraw-Hill) were developed and marketed, and the incestuous relationship between the companies publishing direct instruction reading programs and the panelists reviewing proposals submitted under what was then called the Reading Excellence Act. Since then, researchers like Taylor, Ohanian, Allington, Dudley-Marling, and many others have documented the continuing disastrous effects of Reading First. In late 2006, the Office of the Inspector General investigated the Reading First application process and discovered "a pattern of corruption and mismanagement that is an insult to everyone who takes literacy education seriously." The investigation, said the NCTE, "tells a story of how individuals in powerful positions manipulated the law to enforce a formulaic version of reading instruction skewed by their own view of scientifically based reading research" (NCTE 2006).

At the same time, however, the costs of not participating, as a 2007 *New York Times* story reports, are enormous. The Madison, Wisconsin, district's decision to reject Reading First's direct instruction mandates in favor of a balanced literacy approach to reading cost the district $2 million in federal funds; the same story notes that the New York City Schools chose to adopt direct instruction because it could not afford to lose the $34 million associated with the decision (Schemo 2007).

Certainly, yes, NCLB and Reading First do not apply to higher education. But in the Spellings Commission Report on the Future of Higher Education, a document called *A Test of Leadership* (analyzed in chapter 3), there is ample evidence of what NCTE higher education liaison Paul Bodmer calls a "beltway consensus" around a story about higher education: Universities aren't accountable for what students learn, and they don't make what they do know about their success (or lack thereof) with questions about learning transparent so that the broader public understands them (Bodmer 2007). Since the appointment of Undersecretary for Higher Education Sarah Martinez Tucker (also a member of the Spellings Commission) in January 2007, the Education Department (ED) has begun to speak publicly about changes to its relationship with accrediting agencies and post-secondary institutions.[1] Traditionally, these agencies have urged institutions to establish outcomes and assessment methodologies for assessing those outcomes that make sense for the institution. As another *Inside Higher Education* story noted, "accreditors have primarily focused their judgment of institutions' quality on whether an individual college is showing progress" (Lederman 2007h), and have emphasized that long-term gains in the areas of process and professional development are as important (if not more important) than showing the agencies the results of any assessment.

But the Spellings Report noted that this focus on process, not product, was not producing reliable evidence attesting to institutional accountability.

In early January 2007, the ED official who oversaw accreditation agencies left his position. In mid-January 2007, the ED initiated a process to make changes to the rules governing the higher education accreditation process that would enable the ED to legally regulate that process through accreditation agencies. Initially, the ED outlined a desire to have institutions create norm-referenced assessments across similar colleges and universities (using criteria that were not determined)—in other words, "to judge how well individual colleges are educating their students by comparing them to similar institutions" (Lederman 2007c). They also wanted accrediting agencies to work with the institutions under their auspices to "agree to a core set of student achievement measures, both quantitative and qualitative, focused on those things the institutions have in common, and also on an acceptable level of performance for certain of those measures" (Lederman 2007c).

The ED has already taken steps of their own to initiate this kind of data collection. They are on their way to developing a system called "Huge IPEDS" (or Integrated Postsecondary Education Data System), an online system that would cull data about how colleges and universities gather data about "accountability" on their campuses (e.g., whether they use the National Survey of Student Engagement, the Collegiate Learning Assessment, or other national surveys administered locally on college/university campuses), and then would potentially make that data nationally available. Between March and June 2007 the ED and accrediting agencies attempted to negotiate the rules by which they would discuss accreditation through the ED and the Council on Higher Education Accreditation (CHEA), a separate accrediting body. In June 2007 these negotiations failed, likely leaving the ED free to write their own rules governing this process. As a February 2007 *Inside Higher Education* story noted, the ED has proceeded with this strategy over the strenuous objections of the accrediting agencies and other higher education experts (Lederman 2007c); the ED's goal seems to be to get these regulations in place by July 2008, just six months before the Bush administration leaves office.

So we have a choice. We can sit and wait to see what happens, hoping that the stories that we want to advance (whatever those stories are) about writing and writers are heard, or at least that the stories that we tell (or want to) are ignored by those who have the potential to change them. Certainly that is an option. However, it is probably not the most prudent option, since the likelihood that the glaring light of accountability and assessment will be focused on colleges from the regional or national level seems quite likely. But through this threat—and others to which individual WPAs and writing instructors can doubtless point—is formidable, we need not see it necessarily as a cause for alarm, but as a moment of opportunity. As the introduction to a popular 1970s television show said each week, "We have the technology." We have the brains, the know-how, and the tools. By changing stories at the local level and then working outward to our communities and with our colleagues, we can make a difference. *The Activist WPA* attempts to meet the challenge of changing stories—of reframing discussions—head-on by developing strategies for WPAs and writing instructors to engage in this work.

PERSONAL PRINCIPLES

As I suggested earlier, one of the lessons that I take away from the work of Robert Coles is the connection between personal stories, personal *principles*, and the actions that individuals take based on those principles. Regardless of the theories through which we work as WPAs or writing instructors, what we do is always rooted in *our* emotions, *our* ambitions, *our* goals. In fact, this understanding of individual motivation is also central to the work of the Industrial Areas Foundation (IAF), one of the primary research sites for this book. As Ernesto Cortes, Edward Chambers, and other organizers with the IAF point out, *all* change-making work starts from the individual. "For IAF leaders, the root of 'personal being' is not only understanding feelings in themselves and others, but in coming to terms with their own fundamental self-interest, and then learning to act on it," writes Mary Beth Rodgers, who chronicled the work of IAF organizers in Texas. "IAF leaders . . . believe that involvement with major political events can help both the spiritual and psychological integration of self—through a connection with other people and a mastery of skills and knowledge. But in their view, people can't do that until they come to terms with their own self-interest and their relationship with other people" (Rodgers 1990, 63–64). Change starts with individual principles—from an individual's anger, passions, and (a concept uncomfortable to many academics, including me) *emotions*. It's about understanding one's self, and then connecting with others around one's own interests; ultimately, these connections lead to change-making movements.

Principle Is to Theory as Foundations Are to Buildings

In *The Courage to Teach*, Parker Palmer describes the difference between the divided and undivided teacher. "In the undivided self," he says, "every major thread of one's life experience is honored, creating a web of coherence and strength. . . . Such a self . . . is able to make the connections on which good teaching depends" (Palmer 1998, 15). This is one manifestation of the "spiritual and psychological integration of self"; in Parker's view, it is absolutely essential to becoming a good teacher. The undivided self brings meaningful connection—to subject, to students, to the work (Palmer 1998, 15–18). The divided self, alternatively, distances herself from others because she harbors parts of herself *from* others.

What Palmer calls "the undivided self" is what I think of as a person working from principle. The undivided self is one who can traverse the connection between her own emotions, feelings, experiences and the work of the classroom—and who can elegantly and eloquently connect those things. Others whose ideas are central to this book have written beautifully and extensively about it, too—for Paulo Freire, for instance, it is the process of conscientization, the awareness of the relationships between one's self and the world, and the unfinished and constantly developing nature of that self. For bell hooks it is a pedagogy of the "whole person," one that brings together life and classroom practices. Mary Rose O'Reilley, too, testifies to the importance of this whole person, drawing on Buddhist, Quaker, and Catholic teachings to argue for the importance of being "present"—aware of one's state of being, fully alive and in the moment—for teachers (O'Reilley 2005a, 57–76). Dale Jacobs and Laura Micciche make the case that "the personal and the professional are always interconnected, making the commonplace idea that emotion is solely 'personal' an untenable and insufficient claim because it fails to consider the way emotion refuses to be contained in our 'personal' lives" (Jacobs and Micciche 2003, 6). Dawn Skorczewski, too, suggests that *all* teaching work is rooted in emotion, in the lived experience of the teacher. "We need to look no further than the places that most offend, frustrate, or annoy us . . . to find clues for how to read our personal ideology as it presents itself in our students' work," she writes (Skorczewski 2005, 7). Our identities—as teachers, as professionals, as people living and moving in the world—are constructed on top of our emotional experiencing of ourselves, and ourselves in relation to one another (130).

But as absolutely central as emotion is to our identities as teachers, our work with students, and the very identities that we have constructed for ourselves as professionals, the role of emotion in composition's professional literature has long been a subject of somewhat uncomfortable discussion. Joseph Harris suggests that the discussion of emotion's appropriateness might, in fact, be rooted in the split which became evident at the 1966 Dartmouth conference between a model that positioned English (and writing) as a subject focusing on "the experiences of students and how these are shaped by their uses of language," and one that saw English "as an *academic discipline,* a body of knowledge" (Harris 1997, 2–4, emphasis in original; see also Skorczewski 2005).

Long associated with work that is seen as "expressivist," some have dismissed scholarship that explicitly invokes emotion as overly (and overtly) sentimental, personalized, and even antischolarly. Lad Tobin, whose (funny and engaging) writing blends his personal, emotional responses to the teaching situations he encounters, recounts some of the responses that he has received to his writing: "Several years ago I submitted a piece to a scholarly journal. . . . While one outside reader praised it for the clarity and honesty of the voice, the other rejected it saying, 'I not only hate this article; I also hate this author'" (Tobin 2004, 2). As Tobin notes, there are "a significant number of readers out there who think that confessional writing and personal anecdotes have no place in academic writing" (2). Peter Elbow, too, has written about the struggles that he has encountered in writing about himself in his academic writing. In the early 1980s, Elbow says, his blend of the personal and the "academic" (that is, the subject of writing) "began to be labeled 'expressivist,' 'romantic,' and 'individualist,' and characterized not just as passé, but as deeply flawed from an intellectual and political point of view. . . . By the late '80s, I was seen as a prime exemplar of a theory and philosophy of writing judged to be suspect or even wrong-headed by most of the dominant scholars in the important scholarly journals" (Elbow 2000a, xvi).

Others have explored suggestions that invoking the personal can pull attention away from research and focus it on the researcher (Brandt 2001); call the research into question because of its link to the personal (Cushman 2001; Villanueva 2001); focus an uncomfortable gaze on the researcher (Cushman 2001; Villanueva 2001), or invoke values that are have traditionally not been welcomed within the realm of scholarship (Gere 2001). Ellen Cushman summarized the squishy-feeling-in-the-stomach that is associated with "personal" work when she explained that

The politics of self-disclosure often undermine the good intentions of the personal-as-political movement. The politics of self-disclosure center around the social and cultural forces that press certain individuals to "bare all" and press other individuals to closet themselves, all because their stories are not valued as consumable "goods." The politics of self-disclosure both facilitate and mitigate against particular types of agency in personal narratives by saturating these narratives with greater or lesser economic, moral, and cultural worth. (Cushman 2002, 57)

Parker Palmer and Mary Rose O'Reilley, among others, suggest that this dismissive attitude toward subjective, personal, and emotional experiences are deeply rooted in the nature of the contemporary academy, noting that one of its results is an artificial separation between personal experience and professional work (Palmer 1998, 50–56; O'Reilley 2005b, 84–88). Stemming from Enlightenment epistemologies, in this mode, "truth [is] something that we can achieve only by disconnecting ourselves, physically and emotionally, from the thing we want to know," because if we get too close to it our knowledge of it—perhaps even our feelings about it—will contaminate our perceptions of the thing, and perhaps even the thing itself (Palmer 1998, 51–53). Intellectually and in terms of professional acculturation, this separation has made it more comfortable for many academics (me among them) to operate publicly in the realm of ideas or theoretical frameworks—where we discuss and question our theories or apply them to questions—than in world of principles, which are linked closely to emotion and personal lived experience.

In addition to focusing in the importance of considering emotion because of its role in the classroom, the arguments advanced in these books and articles also make a compelling case for why it is so important for WPAs to begin from principle, emotion, and experience. WPA work is often is shaped by the answers of our institutions and colleagues to the three key questions I've outlined above: How are students' literacies defined when they enter our classes? What literacies should be developed in those classes? How should those literacies be assessed when students leave our classes? These questions (implicitly or explicitly) underscore situations that WPAs initiate and react to—decisions to implement everything from new placement methods to different class sizes, classroom or overall curriculum requirements, and hiring practices. Part of WPA work involves operating successfully within larger systems, as Richard Miller has suggested (1998). This means, of course, acting within the dominant frame around academic work—the one that separates emotion and experience. Imagine for an instant making an emotional appeal to reduce class sizes, or to hire more qualified instructors, or to change a placement method, and you'll see what I mean. At the very best, such an appeal seems implausible; at worst, it seems disastrous. We know that we need to work from theory and research—theories about everything from writing development to student learning to structuring classes and curriculum.

But that theory must stand on a foundation of principle, of emotion—without it, the argument is literally "academic." Principle is the foundation upon which theories are built, and theories "work"—they resonate with those who enact them—because they reflect the principals of those who are doing the enacting. This is the point made by Diana George in her introduction to *Kitchen Cooks, Plate Twirlers, and Troubadours*:

> Some storytelling is necessary if we are to pass on more than theory or pedagogical and administrative tactics to those who come after us. . . . [Writing program administration] is a job and we are workers whose lives are often not so very separate from the things that concern us in our home and intellectual lives. It may be equally important to understand that what we do in these jobs is as figured by our cultural and social histories as by the institutional and economic restraints we confront daily. (George 1999, xii–xiii)

Principles are political—they have meaning and consequence for the individual who holds them, and individuals form principled groups when they align themselves with others who share those principles. Teacher Rebecca Akin writes about the process of enacting principles into practice when she discusses moving from learning about principled practice in her teacher education program at Mills College to a position as a classroom teacher:

> The teaching [in the program] itself was guided by these principles, so that rather than simply being talked about in their teaching, the principles were lived. The impact of such modeling was extraordinarily powerful. The principles became mine because I was immersed in them, I had to grapple with them; they pushed my thinking and my way of understanding the world until finally I not only understood them, but I understood why they mattered. . . . [When I became a teacher], instead of a repertoire of formulaic responses or prescriptions for what to do, however, what I developed was a beginning yet firm foundation that itself would continue to grow and deepen over the years— a frame that helped guide my thinking, questions, dilemmas, uncertainties, emotions, doubts, beliefs, learning, decisions, and actions. (Akin 2005, xxi, emphasis added)

Akin is describing a way of bringing together her own principles with those of her program (through "grappling") and then using those as a foundation for her theoretical work regarding the classroom. Like Akin, Keith Miller and Jennifer Santos argue that assignments where teachers fail to ask students to examine their own principles are akin to "prod[ding] students to explore the many floors in the multi-story dwellings that students call home without ever asking them to examine the foundations of the building. But if students don't analyze the foundation, they may never understand how to design and furnish their own houses" (Miller and Santos 2005, 63). The same holds true for instructors and WPAs, as well: if we don't understand the foundations (and the changes they can make over time) upon which our work is built and operate from those foundations, we will not bring the "undivided" attention that Palmer cites as the most essential element of good teaching.

PRINCIPLES AND LIVED EXPERIENCE

If the work of changing stories is rooted in principle, then the question that remains is how one *finds* one's principles. Certainly, there are compositionists and WPAs (like those cited above) who have both discovered and written about principles that shape their work. There are also others—like me—who are not as experienced in writing about the experiences that led us to develop our principles. And yet, articulating our principles begins with ourselves, our lived experiences. As Coles and others point out, these principles are rooted in stories that individuals tell, stories that come together to constitute that individual's reality. Finding principle, then, begins with considering experience—Cortes and Skorzcewski are among those who suggest considering *strong* experience, experience that affects us emotionally and makes us *feel* (and perhaps think) about things. These experiences constitute the roots of our passion, anger, fear, and beliefs—and from them extend our strongest beliefs, beliefs that must constitute the core of story-changing work. After all: if it doesn't *really* matter to us, why should we expect it to be important for others? "You don't just discuss what people do, or their ideology or the theology of their actions," says IAF organizer Ernesto Cortes. "You must go deeper. Ultimately you must get to the level of how people *feel* about what they do. You want to understand the sources of their anger, or their love, or their interest in something beyond themselves" (Rodgers 1990, 60).

My own experiences of education certainly constitute a central core of the principles from which I operate. Until I arrived in college, I saw and felt myself largely as a school failure. My grades, especially in science and math courses, were terrible (low Cs and a fair number of Ds, with the occasional interim F that I always managed to bring up to a D). I struggled enormously in math, neither understanding core concepts of arithmetic (much less higher math, like algebra) nor being able to find teachers who were willing to believe that my struggles were anything but my own fault. I failed to score highly enough on a variety of standardized tests to gain entrance to talented and gifted programs and schools. But although I was raised by a single-parent mother (like so many of my classmates in early 1970s Albuquerque), I hardly fit the definition of an "at risk" student. There was plenty of reading and writing in my house; we lived in a comfortable, middle-class neighborhood down the street from the University of New Mexico; and I ultimately attended a small, private high school (where I performed poorly in many classes, as above).

On the other hand, my perception of myself, my experience *as* a student, was inconsistent. In many ways I felt I was a failure, and some of my grades and test scores fueled that sense with empirical evidence. But through other factors—my bookshelf full of hard-boiled detective novels, stories that I wrote and filed away in that same bookshelf, and some of the schoolwork I did in classes I liked (history and English)—I think that I knew if I could get out of Albuquerque, I could reinvent myself and construct a new story about myself as a student and a person, one that didn't feel like it had one foot firmly rooted in a sense of myself as a failure. When I left high school (a year early) for college I took advantage of this opportunity. I would say that I never looked back, but that's not really true. I did become a more successful student in college—I had a wonderful experience majoring in history, political science, and extracurricular rabble-rousing, and got respectable if not outstanding grades in the process. But I never lost the sense of being a student with what Lad Tobin calls a "fake ID" (Tobin 2004, 95). That's why, when I finished college, I wiped my hands of the experience of academic study and proceeded into a variety of jobs that I thought would make returning to formal education unnecessary: work as a bookseller and editor; as a teacher of neighborhood history in St. Paul elementary schools; as an arts administrator. After four years of toil in the nonprofit ghetto, though, I was told (by a respected arts administrator offering advice on how I could get a different, better, job) that I needed a master's degree. And so, much to my surprise, I went back to school—and back to confront that dormant sense of failure that wound through my personal story of studenthood.

During the spring of my first year in graduate school, I applied for a teaching position for the following year at General College (GC). As part of my interview, Terry Collins, then the WPA at GC, asked me a question that in some ways became an integral part of my story as a graduate student: "Tell me about a time that you failed." And while the empirical reality of that story might not look like failure to others, it allowed me identify what failure felt like in my own experience—and perhaps more important, to understand how crummy the sense of feeling like a failure can be.

In graduate school I was able to take courses in communication studies, composition, and education that helped me to put my anger and self-interest into broader contexts. But these courses would have meant considerably less had they not been coupled with experience teaching in GC. Founded in the 1930s, GC was originally a college for working adults where classes were held at night and on the weekends so that they could pursue a college degree. By the time I arrived in 1990, GC was a nondegree granting unit, a college for students who had been labeled "underprepared" by the university where they would take smaller classes, receive the benefits of extensive academic advising, and fulfill many of their general education requirements. Nowhere was the college's responsibility for "developmental" education taken more seriously than in composition. Learning to teach in GC's two-course "basic writing" sequence, conceiving of students as anything but incredibly capable and intelligent wasn't an option. Developing a course that was anything less than a serious space for students to do the real work of writing also wasn't even on the radar. My own experiences before college had started me thinking about the nature of "literacy" and "numeracy"—about how they were defined, and how people were labeled "literate" or "illiterate" and why. In graduate courses, I was learning about how communication systems (especially language) reflected and perpetuated ideologies of the cultures in which they were developed; those systems that emerged as dominant inevitably were linked to hegemonic interests in those cultures. While my graduate research was largely focused on historical questions, I was of course thinking about the students with whom I was working in GC. They were labeled "basic writers"—but wasn't that label a manifestation of contemporary definitions of literacy and education (which themselves were forms of communication)? And didn't that label spring from students' previous educational experiences that might have felt to them as crummy and confusing as some of mine did to me?

GC was where I learned to pull these threads of my experience and my intellectual work together to use them as a foundation for my teaching, to draw on my own anger not to fuel outward acts of rage but as a source of empathy and, even more importantly, the starting point for action. In GC, I learned to combine intellectual knowledge developed in classes and conversation with personal experience and become what Palmer calls an "undivided self." I started to understand (though I wouldn't have used these terms at the time) that, for me, teaching was an activity that I could try to perform—consciously, reflectively, and reflexively—to do some good in the world. My experiences as a student and teacher also sit at the core of my passion and anger—the stuff that propels people forward mentioned by Cortes and others (e.g., Taylor 1998). But the explanation of these stories demonstrates another point; stories serve as connections between individual experiences and broader cultures and communities (e.g., White 1978; Brown et al. 2005). This is what Larry Prusack refers to as the "social bonding" function of stories (Prusack 2005, 25).

These experiences also lead to principles which I try to enact in my work as a teacher, a WPA, and a human being: *tikkun olam*, or working to make the world a better place (a principle that stems from my experiences as a Jew), and the concept of prophetic pragmatism. Discussed in chapter 6, both of these principles share three common factors: a commitment to changing things for the better here and now through consensus-based, systematic, thoughtful processes that take into consideration the material contexts and concerns of all involved; a compulsion to be reflexive and self-questioning about this work so as to consider how all involved are taking into account those material conditions; and a constant commitment to ongoing, loud, sometimes messy dialogue among all participants in change-making work that ensures that everyone is heard and, hopefully, represented. When I was asked to tell a story about a time that I failed I could repeat a story about my sense of myself as a frequently failing student that (theoretically at the time, and I hope in practice) allowed me to form connections to other students who sometimes had the same sense of themselves. In a sense, then, these stories (and the language used to represent them) serve as the "code words" mentioned by Hertog and McLeod, phrases (and explanations) that extend out to broader meanings and more extended tropes that reinforce existing frames.

Because of the particular nature of these frames that I enact through my understanding of these principles, I am also led back to the stories that opened this chapter. In particular, I am led back to stories about writing and writers that do not jibe with my own experiences as a writing instructor and WPA, stories that do not resonate the with the optimistic, dialogical, reflexive, and change-making practices that are at the core of principles that I embrace. At the same time, as one who embraces these principles, I am intellectually and emotionally compelled by them to engage in the work represented in this book. I am compelled to try to do something to address what I see as a problem, that composition instructors and WPAs sometimes struggle to bring together what Llewellyn calls "strategies" and "ideals" that are essential for changing stories about out work as writing instructors and about the students who populate our classes. Because we sometimes are not able to bring together strategies and ideals effectively, we have also sometimes struggled to try to insert these stories into public discussions about writers and writing. In the best of situations these struggles are merely frustrating

(the colleagues who tell us, "My students can't write . . . ");
in the worst, they have the potential to profoundly affect the
authority that we are able to exercise in our programs (the institution whose administration dictates curriculum, placement, or
assessment). We need strategies that are connected to our ideals
and ideals that are enacted in strategies.

The first step in connecting ideals and strategies to change
stories is to understand the roots of the struggles that compositionists and WPAs currently face. In chapter 2, I'll dig into this
back story through an examination of the American jeremiad,
especially as it was enacted through American pragmatism.
This story is foundational to America's national identity and
especially to education (including my own, as indicated in the
principles of prophetic pragmatism). Pragmatism's essential
tenets—its fundamental optimism regarding human nature
and human intelligence, its emphasis on method and strategy,
and its belief that humans could work methodically to advance
progress—have become so deeply ingrained in the American
consciousness that Cornel West refers to them as central to
"America['s] religion" (West 1989, 17). They are part of the
"commonsense" narrative about the way that things are and the
way that they work. But because of the "commonsense" nature
of pragmatism and the principles at its very core, this narrative is currently being used for a variety of purposes. Educators
draw from tenets of pragmatism to make the case that our
work is essential for preparing students for participation in the
American democracy, and that we understand best how to enact
this preparation. On the other hand, critics of education draw
on those same tenets to frame another story, that educators
(especially college educators) do not understand the nature of
democracy and, as a result, do not know how to prepare students for participation in democracy. On the third hand, progressive social activists (like those whom I observed to develop
the strategies described here) draw on and adapt pragmatism's
tenets for the strategies that they use to try to affect change. If
we want to build different stories, to construct different tropes

and narratives and shift frames in ways that balance *strategies* and *ideals*, it is therefore essential to understand pragmatism and the progressive pragmatic jeremiad as foundational to the stories that we tell and create.

2
LOOKING BACKWARD

What we don't talk about much, and what leads to some of
the fatigue that we feel, is the fact that during . . . period[s]
of basic change, we have to learn how to challenge and
change some of our background assumptions, some of the
stories, some of the deeply ingrained ways in which we see
the world. . . . We have to find ways to surface some of our
assumptions and narratives, and reflect on them, often in
communities and groups, in order to figure out how we can
productively work with them and constructively challenge
what everyone "knows" to be true.

John Seeley Brown (2005, 55)

Stories serve a variety of purposes. Most compelling for the
immediate purposes of this book, they shape our own and others' understandings of the work of writing instruction, especially
concerning three questions that are central to that work:

How should students' literacies be defined when they come into com-
position classes?

What literacies should composition classes develop, how, and for
what purpose?

How should the development of students' literacies be assessed at the
end of these classes?

In chapter 1, I suggested that actions taken based on
responses to these questions reflect tropes, "movement[s]
from one notion of the way things are related to another
notion, and a connection between things so that they can be
expressed in a language that takes account of the possibility of
their being expressed otherwise" (White 1978, 2, emphasis in
original). The range of these tropes—their representations of
"what things are" and the manner of their extension to other

representations of what things are—are delimited by frames, "organizing principles that are socially shared and persistent over time, that work symbolically to meaningfully structure the social world" (Reese 11). The staying power of these tropes and frames come from their abilities to tap into and work through code concepts—words and ideas—that carry particular meanings (interpretations) and are linked to issues that also extend from and are related to the frame (Reese; Hertog and McLeod 2001). The more stable the association between a concept and a meaning and the tighter the link to the frame, the more the concept is seen as "natural," "taken for granted," and "common sense."

If writing instructors or WPAs want to affect stories—to have some voice in the frames that surround our work and the tropes that emanate from those frames regarding our classes and students—we must develop strategies situated in and reflecting our ideals to shape those frames and tropes. But before we can affect that change, as the quote from John Seeley Brown in the epigraph to this chapter illustrates, we first need to dig into those common sense ideas, the "assumptions and narratives [that] everyone 'knows' to be true." As I discussed in chapter 1, I believe that some of these assumptions and narratives come from the personal principles from which we work, principles that both fuel that work and shape the ways in which we understand it.

These assumptions and narratives also come from the systems in which we work. Regardless of the degree of overlap we see between personal and institutional narratives, the fact is that as educators, WPAs, and writing instructors are always also part of larger bureaucracies, as Richard Miller has persuasively argued (Miller 1998, *passim* 4–9;193–216). That bureaucracy is underscored by long-entrenched assumptions and approaches, what David Tyack and Larry Cuban call "the basic grammar of schooling" (quoted in Miller 1998, 22) that forms the conceptual underpinnings of school and forms the roots of every decision from how a schedule is made to what subjects are taught to what counts as "learning" (22–23).

This is especially true of the "grammar" of American education, a version of the American jeremiad formulated during
the Progressive Era, the period between 1898 and 1920. As
it has been explicated by historian Sacvan Bercovitch, the
American jeremiad posits that America—as a nation of chosen
people endowed (by God) with a mission of exceptionalism—
is always progressing toward the achievement of a virtuous
democracy. This is the nation's errand. However, the wilder-
ness into which that errand is pursued is rife with potential for
declension—individuals or groups who do not embrace the
values of the virtuous democracy, or impediments like disease
and poverty. But rather than see these elements as detractions,
they are incorporated as "affirmations" and "exultations" of
the jeremiad, because they are seen as "corrective" obstacles to
be overcome (Bercovitch 1978, ix–9). The American jeremiad,
says Bercovitch, "was the ritual of a culture on an errand—
which is to say, a culture based on a faith in process. . . . Its
function was to create a climate of anxiety that helped release
the restless 'progressivist' energies required for the success of
the venture" (23).

The Progressive Era version of this jeremiad has served as
an enduring frame surrounding stories about the purpose of
education in the United States. Through it, education is seen as
an essential training ground for preparing students for participation in the democracy. But because of the porous and flexible nature of the progressive pragmatic jeremiad, it supports
multiple, conflicting stories about how that purpose should be
accomplished. Some versions have invested teachers (including
WPAs and writing instructors) with authority to develop curriculum and instruction intended to prepare students for participation in a democracy. But others support charges that teachers
are failing in this responsibility and should have their authority—their agency—removed because they neither understand
the nature of the democracy, nor have the correct methods for
preparing students as participants. If WPAs or writing instructors want to change stories about writers and writing, it is vital

for us to understand how this jeremiad has been developed and used by those espousing seemingly contradictory positions.

OUR GRAMMAR: THE PRAGMATIC/PROGRESSIVE JEREMIAD

The central principles of the progressive pragmatic jeremiad that forms some of the "grammar" of American schooling stem from what Cornel West refers to as "the American religion" of pragmatism (1989, 17), especially as it was enacted during the Progressive Era. Historians pointed to progressivism and the Progressive Era as central foundations for the development of (then) contemporary culture. Historian Douglas Tallack notes that the Progressive Era saw "a broad reorientation of thought away from the chaos and inequities of 19th century laissez-faire liberalism to toward modern, progressive liberalism" (Tallack 1991, 147). Similarly, historian John Chambers writes that "modern America was born" in this period, and "we are heirs to many of the institutions, attitudes, and problems of the Progressive Era" (Chambers vii). Historians of education have also noted the profound influence that progressive approaches to education have had on contemporary schooling.

The progressive jeremiad was firmly situated in the context of late-nineteenth/early-twentieth century culture, a period in which the United States was changing dramatically. Most of these changes can be traced back to seismic shifts that facilitated communication. The invention of the telegraph, the completion of the transcontinental railroad, developments in large-scale printing and circulation, the spread of movies and of radio, the arrival of millions of immigrants—all led the generation of Americans who had come of age during the mid- and late-nineteenth century to understand that dramatic changes were occurring (e.g., Hofstadter 1955; Susman 1984; Czitrom 1983). In the context of these rapid social changes, the group of writers and thinkers known as progressives and pragmatists emerged as leading intellectual lights.

The jeremiad embraced by the social, political, and intellectual activists of this period comes out of this context of rapid social and political change. It is rooted in what West refers to as the "Emersonian theodicy" of optimistic faith in the power of the right kind of individuals to affect the right kind of change through the right kinds of processes (West 1989, 15). Progressive pragmatists, especially John Dewey, injected into the pragmatic/progressive jeremiad three crucial tenets. First was a belief in the power of individuals to enact critical intelligence that would enhance their circumstances (and, therefore, the collective circumstances of the nation). Critical intelligence involved engaging in informed reflection; demystifying the components of knowledge-making processes so that they could be accessed (and employed) by the largest numbers of people possible; and applying these processes and intelligences to overcome obstacles standing in the way of the achievement of the virtuous democracy (see West 1989, 70–76; Carey 1989, 23–35). Second was the belief that, through the application of critical intelligence, individuals could collectively determine the best methods through which to achieve the betterment of individual (and therefore collective) circumstances. Third was a profound confidence in community, defined as entities formed by individuals of like minds, to attend to the concerns of one another.

On its face, progressive pragmatism reflected the optimism and faith in individuals that was at the core of the pragmatic jeremiad. It added to that narrative the idea that individually rooted work, applied through scientifically sound methods developed and guided by experts, could overcome obstacles that stood in the way of the nation's progress. For progressive pragmatists, two obstacles were especially problematic. First was the search for capital "T" truth. This misdirection of human energies would pull toward an unusable, destructive past (a past that sought perfection, rather than emphasizing the questlike nature of the jeremiad that, as Bercovitch has identified, is a central feature *of* the American jeremiad). Dewey noted that

> the chief characteristic trait of the pragmatic notion of reality is precisely that no theory of Reality in general . . . is possible or

needed . . . it finds that "reality" is a denotative term, a word used
to designate indifferently everything that happens. . . . Speaking
summarily, I find that the retention by philosophy of a notion of a
Reality feudally superior to the events of everyday occurrence is the
chief source of the increasing isolation of philosophy from common
sense and science. (quoted in West 1989, 94)

Rather, Dewey asserted, "truth [was] a species of the
good . . . the procedures that produce warranted assertions
are themselves value-laden and exemplary of human beings
working in solidarity for the common good" (quoted in West
1989, 100).

A second element of declension in the progressive pragmatic
jeremiad took the form of social and cultural elements that
could detract from individuals' innate desires to contribute to
the formation of a public sphere. That is, while pragmatic progressives believed that there was a "public, . . . [a] large body of
persons having an interest in the consequences of social transac-
tions," (quoted in West 1989, 104) they also believed that any
number of social, cultural, political, and economic forces could
assert unwanted influence on the individuals that comprised
this public, thus ultimately affecting the actions that they would
take regarding its shape. As West notes, progressive pragmatists
identified these challenges in the very communication tech-
nologies that propelled the Progressive Era:

The major obstacles to creating a public sphere—a discursive and
dialogical social space where in the various "publics" can find
common ground—are the proliferations of popular cultural diver-
sions from political concern such as sports, movies, radio, cars; the
bureaucratization of politics; the geographical mobility of persons;
and most important, the cultural lag in ideas, ideals, and symbols
that prohibits genuine communication. (West 1989, 105)

These communication developments also contributed to economic circumstances that presented the threat of declension,
the growth of big business. Progressives believed that factories,

railroads, oil companies, and other industries whose growth was in part facilitated by increased mobility ran amuck, amassing enormous wealth for a few individuals on the backs of the labor of many. The explosion in industrial manufacturing that had led to the development of such businesses was propelled by and perpetuated enormous inequality—poor working conditions, deplorable living conditions, lack of attention to social issues such as poverty and health care (e.g., Noble, 1985, 27–40; Carey, 1997, 70–75). Within the progressive pragmatic jeremiad, the only possibility for overcoming the declensions represented by these threats lay in the application of individual creative intelligence to the development of systems designed to regulate what Chambers refers to as the perception of "unrestricted individualism, the unregulated marketplace, and the self-regulated society" (Chambers 1992, 276). Through this intelligence, individuals could study these problems scientifically and develop systematic processes through which they could be addressed. In fact, it was these processes (even more than their results) that were essential for moving the democracy forward.

Evidence of these efforts during the Progressive Era abound. Journalist Lincoln Steffens took on corruption in local government; Upton Sinclair, journalist and later politician, tackled issues of workers' rights and workplace safety; photographer Lewis Hine turned his lens on child welfare and living conditions of the poor; academics associated with pragmatism, the intellectual wing of progressivism, developed methods that would enable the "scientific" study of social phenomena that would provide a basis for reformers' efforts. Agencies and governmental offices charged with overseeing the development of data and processes for advancing democracy flourished during this period. The Food and Drug Administration and the Federal Trade Commission were among the federal offices founded during this period; numerous laws such as the Keating-Owen Act, which forbade the sale of products manufactured by children from interstate commerce, and the Workman's Compensation Act, which provided protection for workplace injuries, were also passed at the federal level. Individual states also continued to pass laws requiring mandatory school attendance, a movement initiated in the mid-nineteenth century. The assumption was that, through the development and execution of properly developed and managed processes (of education, regulation, research, and so on) individuals could—and would—come together to address larger social inequities, regardless of the cultures and interests that they brought to their efforts. Educational historian Douglas McKnight cites a speaker from the 1889 National Education Association conference whose presentation reflected this sense of mission:

> The school life, brief as it is, may reasonably be asked to furnish to the Republic loyal and obedient citizens; to the business world, men with a courage and a grip that will not too easily let go in the pushing affairs of trade; to the social life, an ease and graced of manners, a strength of self-reliance, which shall put each in possession of his full powers for his own building and for the advancement for his associates. (quoted in McKnight 2003, 89, emphasis added)

PROGRESSIVE EDUCATION AND THE PROGRESSIVE PRAGMATIC JEREMIAD

Within this context, progressive educational theory emphasized creating social conditions conducive to educational development rather than providing what we now might refer to as direct instruction. As Dewey explained, education was intended to provide "direction, control, or guidance," but the last word—guidance—"conveys the idea of assisting through cooperation the natural capacities of the individuals guided; control conveys rather the notion of an energy brought to bear from without and meeting some resistance from the one controlled. . . . Control . . . denotes a process by which [the individual] is brought to subordinate his own natural impulses to public or common ends" (Dewey 1916, 23).

Instead, Dewey wrote, education should provide stimulus to direct activity. "[Stimulus] does not simply excite [activity] or stir it up, but directs it toward an object. . . . There is an adaptation of the stimulus and response to each other" (24). Education, Dewey said, provided direction for this stimulus so that it was not "wasted, going aside from the point," or would "go against the successful performance of an act. . . . Direction is both simultaneous and successive," ultimately contributing to the development of critical intelligence that would guarantee the appropriate application of and response to various stimuli (25–29). Education should enable students to become better individuals by cultivating their individual creative intelligence so that they might apply this intelligence to the development of methods designed to overcome potential declensions, obstacles to the nation's progress toward the virtuous democracy.

The problem, as later critics have noted, is that while progressive pragmatists emphasized the profound power of individual creative intelligence to come together and collectively form a virtuous democracy, they also (often explicitly) avoided situating that potential in any specific context. Historian Warren Susman characterizes this as a desire to be "*in* the world but not *of* the world" (1984, 95). Cornel West describes this epistemology in more detail, noting that Dewey's "central concern" was

> to extend the experimental method . . . rather than to discern the social forces and historical agents capable of acting on and actualizing . . . creative democracy. . . . [Dewey's] distrust of resolute ideological positioning, as in political parties and social movements from below, led him to elevate the dissemination of critical intelligence at the expense of collective insurgency. . . . His gradualism is principally pedagogical in content, and his reformism is primary dialogic in character. He shuns confrontational politics and agitational struggle. The major means by which creative democracy is furthered is through education and discussion. (1989, 102)

The "evasion" of content—that is, the frequent evasion of the specific material (economic) conditions in which the progressive pragmatic jeremiad was developed that is located in pragmatic thinking by West, C. Wright Mills, and others—has left the narrative embedded in this jeremiad open to a variety of applications. Even during the Progressive Era, this porous quality resulted in two primary approaches—one emphasizing the cultivation of critical intelligence by means of inductive, nurturing education, the other making the case that critical intelligence was best imposed from above.

The former approach, labeled by historian Warren Susman as "stewardly" (Susman 1984, 90) and by educational historian David Tyack as "humanitarian" (Tyack 2003, 75), was based on the premise that, guided correctly, everyone's intelligence could be shaped so as to contribute to the achievement of the American democracy. Educators embracing this approach focused on cultivating community through the development of environments where individuals would come to participate in the values seen as essential for the perpetuation of the progressive narrative. This principle was at the core of Dewey's thinking, as he explained in *Democracy and Education*:

> We have seen that the community or social group sustains itself through continuous self-renewal, and . . . this renewal takes place by means of the educational growth of the immature members of the group. By various agencies, unintentional and designed, a society transforms uninitiated and seemingly alien beings into robust trustees of its own resources and ideals. Education is thus a fostering, a nurturing, a cultivating process. . . . We speak of education as shaping, forming, molding activity—that is, a shaping into the standard form of social activity. . . . What is required is a transformation of the quality of experience till it partakes in the interests, purpose, and ideas current in the social group. . . . Beliefs and aspirations cannot be physically extracted and inserted. How then are they communicated? . . . The answer, in general formulation, is: By means of the action of the environment in calling out certain responses. The required beliefs cannot be hammered in; the needed attitudes cannot be plastered on. But the particular medium in which an individual exists leads him to see and feel one thing rather than another; it leads him to have certain plans in order that he may act successfully with others; it strengthens some beliefs and weakens

others as a condition of winning the approval of others. Thus it gradually produces in him a system of behavior, a certain disposition of action. (10–11)

For Dewey, education was the communicative medium where students would come, through conditioning, to understand how to bring their interests into alignment with others'. Not "hammered in," not "plastered on"—the key was developing "behaviors" and "dispositions" that led to assimilation and participation in dominant values and cultures.

While Dewey's work laid out the theoretical principles of the stewardly approach, writers whose style was less obtuse grounded it more fully in practical experience. In *Twenty Years at Hull-House,* Jane Addams (a close friend of Dewey's) described the work of her settlement house through the metaphor of the *Messiah.* Like Dewey, Addams advocated cultivating neighborhood residents toward participation in a common purpose, rather than imposing purpose upon them:

> In a thousand voices singing the Hallelujah Chorus . . . it is possible to distinguish the leading voices, but the differences of training and cultivation between them and the voices in the chorus, are lost in the unity of purpose and in the fact that they are all human voices lifted by a high motive. This is a weak illustration of what a Settlement attempts to do. It aims, in a measure, to develop whatever of social life its neighborhood may afford, to focus and give form to that life, to bring to bear upon it the results of cultivation and training; but it receives in exchange for the music of isolated voices the volume and strength of the chorus. (125)

Addams's vision was one where, no matter their backgrounds, any individual could participate in the "scientific" work through which strategies and solutions that would enable individuals to cope with the challenges and opportunities of everyday life would be developed. She explained that

> the Settlement . . . must be hospitable and ready for experiment. It should demand from its residents a scientific patience in the

accumulation of facts and the steady holding of their sympathies as one of the best instruments for that accumulation. It must be grounded in a philosophy whose foundation is on the solidarity of the human race, a philosophy which will not waver when the race happens to be represented by a drunken woman or an idiot boy. (126)

Books like Frank Thompson's *The Schooling of the Immigrant* (1920) also advanced the argument that schooling should help students come to partake in American cultural values. In 400 pages—and referencing numerous charts, graphs, and diagrams that reflect the progressive emphasis on "scientific study"— Thompson made the case that "persuasion," not "compulsion," should underscore the education of the "foreign born" (16). J. Stanley Brown, superintendent of a Joliet, Illinois high school, also invoked this stewardly, humanitarian approach when he described the "ideal secondary teacher." "The way of approach to the teacher ought to be made easy by him in leading the youth, step to step, to see that his highest interests are served," Brown wrote. "The door to such an approach ought always to be ajar, and the way should grow more and more familiar by use. By this means can the indispensable personal relations between the ideal teacher and the student be preserved" (Brown 1905, 29–30).

All of these educators' work reflects the belief that education, as a communicative medium, could cultivate students' development. Dewey referred to this as cultivating students' "qualities of experience," and *cultivation* of these experiences, rather than *imposition* of them, is one of the central features of the stewardly or humanitarian approach. Within composition and rhetoric education, this approach is also reflected in what James Berlin called the "rhetoric of public discourse" evident in the work of rhetoricians like Fred Newton Scott, Joseph Denney, and Gertrude Buck (who was Scott's student) (Berlin 25–36, 46–50). Within this paradigm the presumption was that language was an interrelationship of "the experience of the external world and what the perceiver brings to this experience" (Berlin 47).

Language instruction, then, was to simultaneously push students to examine their own understandings and to analyze and take into account context, purpose, and audience (Berlin 49–50).[1]

But where stewards emphasized that the virtuous democracy would be achieved through the cultivation of individuals' critical intelligence, a mission that they believed could be accomplished through education, others believed that it was necessary to develop systems and structures to direct that intelligence for individuals. Susman refers to this group as "technocrats" (Susman 1984, 90), Tyack as "interventionists" (Tyack 2003, 75). Rather than cultivating a state where individuals who had come to partake in the values of the culture acted upon those values, technocrats wanted to "make the system work to the profit of the whole nation and its citizens, . . . [a state] directed by an elite of . . . trained and efficient . . . experts" (Susman 1984, 92). The technocratic version of progressivism is most famously represented in the work of journalist Walter Lippmann, who took the stance that only experts could steer the nation and that the individual citizen should have little role in this work. Lippman believed that individual action was based on "pictures in [individual's] heads" that were formed by symbols (Lippmann 1922, 12–29); the ever-increasing array of mass media made available during the first part of the twentieth century offered too many symbols and too wide a range of interpretations. If interpretations differed, then the actions that individuals take might also differ. If that were to be the case chaos would ensue, because the "moral code" of the culture, from which rules governing the culture stem, would not be consistently understood and acted upon by citizens (120–21).

Ensuring that symbols were consistently cultivated and individual action based on those symbols was directed toward the betterment of society and the achievement of progress, Lippman argued, was the work of managing public opinion. Public opinion was to be executed by a group of experts— "some form of expertness between the private citizen and the vast environment in which he is entangled" (378)—who worked from scientific data. But where proponents of the more humanitarian, stewardly approach made the case that individuals should cultivate habits and dispositions that would incline them to participation in progressive values and culture, those working from this more technocratic, interventionist stance believed that individuals would choose to turn their attention elsewhere. The common person, he said, "has neither time, nor attention, nor interest, nor the equipment of specific judgment. It is on [experts], working under conditions that are sound, that the daily administrations of society must rest" (400).

Thus the key was for experts to manage those interpretations *for* individuals. Through communication (including education) experts could propagate responses and cultivate stereotypes which would call out correct interpretations, which would then serve as the basis for correct responses (in journalism Lippmann referred to this [in a positive sense] as "propaganda"). When individuals circulated among groups who shared the same prejudices and acted in those prejudices in similar ways, consensus would be achieved (175). The role of the individual citizen would be only to ensure that the mechanisms by which her public opinion is gathered and acted upon were "sound":

> The private citizen . . . will soon see . . . that [appeals for the "loan of his Public Opinion"] are not a compliment to his intelligence, but an imposition on his good nature and an insult to his sense of evidence . . . he will concern himself about the equity and sanity of the procedure, and even this he will in most cases expect his elected representative to watch for him. He will refuse himself to accept the burden of these decisions. . . . Only by insisting that problems shall not come up to him until they have passed through a procedure, can the busy citizen of a modern state hope to deal with them in a form that is intelligible. (400–401)

In education, this approach is most visible in efforts to tailor educational practices and procedures, as in E. L. Thorndike's work. All response, Thorndike suggested, was the result of conditioning; extending this premise to education, schooling could be seen as a situation for conditioning and it was important that this conditioning be guided by experts. Simple training by repetition would not be adequate—as Thorndike explained, "the repetition of a situation in and of itself has no selective power. . . . The repetition of a situation may change a man as little as the repetition of a message over a wire changes the wire. In and of itself, it may teach him as little as the message teaches the switchboard" (Thorndike 14). But at the same time experts needed to help direct the conditioning occurring in learning response so that what was "true" was legitimized and what was false was not. Additionally, not everyone needed to know the same things, or the same number of things. As Thorndike explained, science had helped sort out "truth and error," "myth and fact" in what people learned (Thorndike 196). At the same time, "the evolution of learning" had led to the capacity to teach (and learn) "equally different things more quickly and pleasantly" (than before). As a result, more people were able to learn more things; for that learning to be useful and productive, a sorting system was necessary.

> At present, the distribution of learning in schools is largely indiscriminate, the active ideal being to have as many children as possible learn as much as possible, with very little regard to who learns what. . . . The benevolent forces work in too great disregard of what people really want. . . . So there is now considerable danger that many individuals will learn much that they cannot enjoy or use for the common good, and that some individuals will fail to learn what they need to make them happy and useful. The scientific study of human nature by the idealists and reformers and the development of finer standards of success in business will, it may be hoped and believed, produce a much better distribution of learning. (Thorndike 196–98)

Here, the function of educators was in part to sort through "fact" and "folly," in part to more efficiently condition learners, and in part to determine who should learn what, for what purposes, and why. In composition and rhetoric, this approach to education is evident in what Berlin refers to as "the efficiency movement," an effort to quantify objectives and learning and apply those to the teaching (and assessment) of writing. This push for quantification also underscores behavioralist models like the ones Mike Rose describes in "The Language of Exclusion: Writing Instruction at the University," models that are "atomistic, focusing on isolated bits of discourse, [are] error centered, and [are] linguistically reductive" (Rose 1985, 343).

But while this approach, especially as it was developed through Thorndike's work, seems distant from the more stewardly, humanitarian one, both approaches are actually rooted in the same progressive pragmatic jeremiad. Both incorporate the notions that the nation is progressing toward the achievement of a virtuous democracy, but that there are threats to the achievement of that goal that can be overcome only with systematic cultivation of critical intelligence through proven methods. The difference—and it is an important difference—lay in the question of method, not substance. Stewards suggested that this nurturing could be cultivated within the individual; technocrats made the case that expert managers should instead sort and manage the process *for* individuals.

MOVING ON: THE PROGRESSIVE PRAGMATIC JEREMIAD AND CONTEMPORARY AMERICA

The importance of the progressive movement in education, itself rooted in this progressive pragmatic jeremiad, is taken as one of the foundational periods in American education. Educational histories routinely cite the importance of the period: Howard Ozmon and Samuel Craver's *Philosophical Foundations of Education* note that "the impact of pragmatism on American education has been considerable. Many schools have implemented elements of pragmatic ideas in one way or another, but this influence is not always consciously connected with the philosophy" (Ozmon and Craver 1995, 149), while John Pulliam and J. J. Van Patten's *History of Education in America* notes that the influence of pragmatism and progressivism, especially as it was interpreted by Dewey, remain a profound influence shaping American education (Pulliam and Van Patten 2007, 48–49). In our own field, the idea that writing instruction contributes to the development of students' "critical intelligence" is a mainstay of the field. "Critical thinking, reading, and writing" is one of the four primary areas of focus in the WPA Outcomes Statement (Writing Program Administrators 2000); a search for research on critical thinking (defined as the ability to engage in reflection, to demystify knowledge to make its acquisition visible, and to apply concepts in a range of contexts) in the CompPile bibliography yields over 200 entries.

But the "evasion of philosophy" in this narrative—that is, pragmatism's emphasis on generalizable methods, solutions, and applications rather than its focus on particular challenges stemming from particular temporal and spatial contexts— makes it available for a variety of purposes. This porous nature of this jeremiad is evident in Geoffrey Nunberg's study of shifts in meaning around words typically associated with progressive politics. Studying the language used to justify progressive programs during the Nixon administration, Nunberg points to what historian Gene Wise has called a "pivotal moment" in the application of this jeremiad, that is, a moment indicating "a threshold of change—a fault-line" (Wise 140). Rather than referencing programs developed through the application of the progressive pragmatic jeremiad as closing gaps in American society and cultivating the critical intelligence necessary to achieve a virtuous democracy that represented the interests of individuals, in the late 1960s and early 1970s Republicans began to argue that these progressive programs were the property of "liberals" and favored their interests *against* the interests of the "common man." According to Nunberg:

> Republicans re[wrote] the old language of [progressivism] in ways that diverted the traditional conflicts between "the people" and "the powerful" into "cultural" resentments over differences in lifestyle and social values. . . . In the course of things, [Republicans]

managed to redefine the distinction between conservatives and liberals, so as to depict liberals as the enemies of the values of "ordinary Americans." (Nunberg 2006, 51)

The shift identified by Nunberg has persisted into the twenty-first century, where this dual purposing of the progressive pragmatic jeremiad persists. As in the 1970s, essential elements of it are today wielded against the traditional allies of progressivism, who are charged with "denying opportunity" or "standing in the way of progress" when they try to argue against the repurposing of the progressive frame. Kathy Emery and Susan Ohanian, for instance, connect the dots from the Republicans' invocation of (language and) values associated with progressivism to "school reform" as it has been enacted in the last 20 years, for instance. First, they point to language that (former Republican Speaker of the House) Newt Gingrich told Republicans to use when describing themselves, words that reflect the values associated with the stewardship tradition described earlier: "active, activist, building, . . . care, children, . . . citizen, . . . common sense . . . liberty . . . opportunity, . . . reform" (Emery and Ohanian 2004, 5). They then locate this language squarely in NCLB. "In the hands of the U.S. Department of Education," they write,

> the very title No Child Left Behind, hijacked from the Children's Defense Fund, has become the moral equivalent of the Pentagon's pacification. . . . [NCLB] means the opposite of what it says. It is a plan . . . to declare public schools failures and accelerate the use of vouchers, turning public education over to private, for-profit firms. It is also a plan to blame the victim: the government declares it's leaving no child behind, so if a kid ends up on the streets after tenth grade, it must be his fault. (Emery and Ohanian 2004, 5–6)

A recent column by conservative columnist George Will also captures this shift. In it, Will takes a term at the center of the progressive narrative, "opportunity," and uses it to flog opponents of school vouchers in Arizona. By denying poor children the "opportunity" to attend private schools with public funds,

Will argues, these opponents are denying them the opportunity to become educated citizens (Will 2007). Embedded in Will's column are elements of the progressive counternarrative that is now being turned against educators through the lens of progressivism. It goes like this: the purpose of school is to prepare students for participation in the democracy, and teachers (and school systems) have long been granted the expertise, within the progressive frame, to tend to this preparation. However, in the last X years (the number of years depends on the argument being advanced), teachers and school systems have begun to fail in their appointed mission; they are not preparing students because they do not understand the nature of the *new* democracy. Educational historian Douglas McKnight observes the same phenomenon in his analysis of the current jeremiads around education:

> Present-day America is perceived as immersed in a moral crisis because of certain cultural conditions. National identity has fractured, resulting in a pervading sense of uncertainty and anxiety about the future. Public schools, as institutions charged with preserving the symbols of national identity and a morality that is the concrete expression of those symbols, have failed and must be reformed. . . . Resolving the crisis is dependent upon schools remembering and transmitting middle-class cultural identity[, but schools are also] fail[ing] in this charge. . . . According to the modern jeremiads, schools, and specifically teachers, no longer direct children through the process of moral transcendence—a state in which each child comes to understand and accept his or her role in society and fulfills this prescribed destiny in a carefully measured manner. (2003, 122–23)

While McKnight notes that this antieducation jeremiad has occurred in cycles throughout American history, the current use of this story about education offers a new twist. As discussed in chapter 1, the Education Department (ED) is currently working through changes to the rule-making process that guide its work with accreditation agencies, who in turn set procedures by which colleges and universities assess their effectiveness. The proposed changes—which seem virtually inevitable—would allow the ED to impose standards for what kinds of assessments are legitimate, what kinds of data must be submitted to demonstrate achievement regarding effectiveness, and how those data would be used to fuel comparisons across institutional categories (also set by the ED). As a respondent to a March 2007 *Inside Higher Education* story about this process wrote:

> In true "not in my backyard" fashion, the same liberals/authoritarians who generally want the government to regulate everything are now saying, "Hold on now" when the government wants to regulate, albeit indirectly, traditional higher education "outcomes". . . . So to my friends in traditional higher education I say, welcome to my nightmare, and a dose of your own medicine. (Bogart 2007)

As this response suggests, the potential for this use of the progressive narrative has always been there, part and parcel of the progressive pragmatic jeremiad. Nunberg notes that "if nothing else, the right has demonstrated how versatile [the narrative associated with this jeremiad] can be connecting threads among programs and policies" (Nunberg 2006, 203). James Gee makes the same point when he notes that

> Literacy always comes with a perspective on interpretation that is ultimately political. . . . In the end, we might say that . . . nothing follows from literacy or schooling. Much follows, however, from what comes with literacy and schooling, what literacy and schooling come wrapped up in, namely the attitudes, values, norms, and beliefs (at once social, cultural and political) that always accompany literacy and schooling. (1996, 38–39)

Hence the problem. For over one hundred years, the left has relied on central elements of progressive pragmatic jeremiad to fuel its work: extending social services to those in need, creating programs and agencies to ensure that treatments and protections were extended equally; developing agencies whose purposes were to ensure that "opportunity"—economic, social, political, and otherwise—was available to all. At the same time, the very porous nature of this jeremiad—its primary emphasis on the development and application of individual critical intelligence through method and process without explicit (or, sometimes, implicit) contextualizing in specific social and material conditions—has made it available for those holding other positions, as well.

Returning to the issue of story-changing, teachers generally and WPAs and writing instructors more specifically have a conundrum. As outlined above, the progressive pragmatic jeremiad is central to the work of American education; certainly, it is often located in some of composition's fundamental tenets. One need look no further than a document like the NCTE "Beliefs about the Teaching of Writing," a document compiled by the NCTE Executive Board (for which a wide range of input from NCTE's members was solicited) as evidence. After its initial assertion that "everyone has the capacity to write, writing can be taught, and teachers can help students become better writers," the document goes on to emphasize that writing is developed through processes guided by instructors and contributed to by individuals, and also shaped by exigencies (NCTE 2004). And while these may seem like commonsense principles, they only seem that way because they at least in part rooted in this narrative, so familiar it feels like an old (comfortable) sweatshirt.

Recall, too, that the staying power of tropes and frames comes from their abilities to tap into and work through code concepts that carry particular meanings. Nunberg's analysis points to a moment where the meanings associated with particular words— "progressive," "liberal," and so on—were shifted to refer to a set of meanings that, while not traditionally associated, were available within the porous nature of the progressive pragmatic jeremiad. If WPAs and writing instructors want to affect the stories shaping what we do—that is, if we want to shape those stories so that we have some agency regarding the three issues that are central to that work (how should students' literacies be defined when they come into composition classes; what literacies should composition classes develop, how, and for what purpose; and how should the development of students' literacies be assessed at the end of these classes), we must consider the frame that we use for that argument.

When we rely on the progressive pragmatic jeremiad, which encompasses both a purpose and methods that are ingrained in the "grammar" of American schooling (and which, as I described in chapter 1, is certainly linked to my own motivating principle of prophetic pragmatism), we must think carefully. This is a porous narrative. It can support a technocractic/behavioralist conception of education (which affects everything from definitions of what writing instruction is, to the authority that instructors have in developing curriculum and instruction) or a notion of education as servitude (which removes most agency from students); it also can support the case that education must support the development of individuals' senses of critical intelligence, including a careful and considered exploration of the material contexts through which that development occurs.

The left's failure to address this dilemma is precisely what has spurred the recent flurry of activity around the concept of framing which I'll discuss in chapters 3 and 5. George Lakoff, perhaps the most prominent proponent of "reframing," has argued that trying to recapture a previously left-serving frame that has been taken over by the right only serves to perpetuate the interests *of* the right, because it perpetuates the frame. At the same time, the left has been woefully terrible at coming up with *new* frames that represent what it *does* believe, not what it *does not* believe. Alan Jenkins, executive director of the Opportunity Agenda, one of many progressive groups attempting to generate a platform for this framing, summarized the problem in a presentation: "Martin Luther King never said 'I have a critique.'" But when the Democratic party "crafted" the message, "Together, America can do better" for its 2006 platform, they hardly captured the American imagination with a vision of the possible. Nunberg quotes a blogger, Wonkette, whose response gets to the heart of the problem: "Now we know where the Democrats stand. . . . They stand for betterness" (2006, 2).

As the analysis in the next chapter illustrates, this problem of language and ideology also forms the framework around the challenge currently faced by educators. A number of influential reports (and news stories like those quoted in chapter 1) invoke the progressive pragmatic jeremiad to make the case that the purpose of education is to prepare students for participation in the democracy, but that that the educational system (especially teachers) are faltering in this mission. Through this same narrative, the state has for the last century also been charged with some degree of responsibility to address failures; thus, these documents invoke solutions that remove agency from teachers and perpetuate stories about students (writers) and content (like writing) that run counter to narratives that are reflected in pedagogical research like that from our field of composition and rhetoric. If we want to change frames and stories about our work and about the subjects that we teach by invoking elements of this jeremiad— saying, for instance, that writing instruction helps prepare students for citizenship in a twenty-first-century democracy (WPA Assessment Statement)—we must do so consciously, understanding the porous nature of the narrative that we are invoking, and think carefully about how our arguments are positioned within it.

3

FRAMING THE PUBLIC
IMAGINATION

*In Arizona, some amazingly persistent and mostly liberal
people are demonstrating the tenacity with which some interests fight to prevent parents of modest means from having
education choices like those available to most Americans. In
1999, Arizona's Supreme Court upheld a program whereby
individuals receive tax credits for donations they make to
organizations that provide scholarships to enable children to
attend private schools, religious and secular. . . . Thousands
of families are on waiting lists for scholarships.*

*In 2000, Arizona opponents of school choice, in a suit
filed by the American Civil Liberties Union, attacked the program in federal court. They failed again. . . . Now, Arizona
opponents of school choice, thirsting for a third defeat, are
challenging what Arizona's legislature enacted last year.
Noting the success of the individual tax credit for scholarship
contributions, the Legislature has authorized corporate donors
a dollar-for-dollar tax credit for contributions to private,
nonprofit school tuition organizations. Opponents of school
choice are trudging back to court where they will recycle twice-
rejected arguments.*

*That is about the control of schools by bureaucrats,
about work rules negotiated by unions and, not least, about
money—not allowing any to flow away from . . . [the public
school lobby].*

George Will

STORIES TOLD ABOUT SCHOOL: THE FAILURE
OF OPPORTUNITY

The column from which this excerpt is drawn illustrates the
ways that elements of the progressive pragmatic jeremiad

contribute to a frame surrounding discussions of education (and writing) in widely read documents, like news stories and policy reports (which are often cited in news stories). In that jeremiad, the purpose of education is to cultivate individuals' critical intelligence so that they can contribute to the development of methods and processes used to overcome obstacles, which will in turn ensure the continued progress of the nation toward the achievement of a virtuous democracy. Code words in this column, though—"[parents of] modest means, education choices, [school] choice, control [of schools by] bureaucrats"— point to a story about how schools (and teachers) are failing in their mission to cultivate or impose this intelligence and the skills that accompany it. Wealthy parents can send their children to other (private) schools that do a better job, but "parents of modest means" are denied choice. Choice is but one element of *liberty* and liberty, the ability to control one's own destiny, is a key feature of the progressive pragmatic jeremiad (because it is necessary for the development and unprovoked application of critical intelligence) (see Hanson 62–63).

Will's column is but one example of the ways that conservatives have used the progressive pragmatic jeremiad in recent years. Since the Progressive Era, education has been identified as a key site for the cultivation of critical intelligence that would enable citizens to locate their place in the jeremiad and thus contribute to the nation's progress toward the virtuous democracy. But as chapter 2 suggests, the emphasis on the development of individual creative intelligence and individually derived processes have made it available for a variety of purposes. Especially as it was developed in the early part of the twentieth century, this narrative was often not situated in specific, material considerations, an elision that led critics like C. Wright Mills to charge that the progressive pragmatic jeremiad separated action from "any realities of modern social structure that might serve as the means for [their] realization" (quoted in West 1989, 127).

In this chapter, I examine how the progressive pragmatic jeremiad has been incorporated into different frames surrounding stories about the purposes of education, and educators' role within those purposes. First, I focus on *A Test of Leadership* and *Ready or Not*, two influential policy reports that frame educators and the educational system as out-of-touch and powerless. Both infer that teachers have no sense of the purpose of their mission or of their roles in executing that mission, and suggest that outside experts must intervene with methods that teachers can use to develop students' critical intelligence. I then briefly examine documents from one of the outside experts to whom these documents allude, ACT. Then I examine news stories about the SAT writing exam that frame educators differently, as knowledgeable and informed professionals. These later news items suggest that teachers not only understand the complexities of twenty-first-century culture, but also understand the complexities of cultivating the multiple critical intelligences that students will need to participate in this culture. Finally, I consider questions about the ways that teachers—WPAs and writing instructors—might define our roles in relation to these frames if we want to engage in the work of changing stories.

FAILING SCHOOLS, FAILING STUDENTS: A TEST OF LEADERSHIP

This idea that education is faltering significantly in its central charge is one of the frames surrounding discussions of teaching that take place in mainstream media (and other sites outside of academe), as many have noted (e.g., Harris 1997; Mortensen 1998; Ohanian). The primary argument embedded in this charge is that schools (and teachers) do not understand the nature of twenty-first-century democracy; this failure of understanding then contributes to the lack of alignment among curriculum and a lack of preparation among students. Within the progressive pragmatic frame, then, it is the state's responsibility to step in and ensure that the system is maintained, or otherwise to find other experts who can do so. This conceptualization of teachers and education is readily apparent in *A Test of Leadership*, the final report of the Spellings Commission on Higher Education. The report illustrates how the Bush administration has faulted education for failing to fulfill the vision of education stemming from the progressive pragmatic jeremiad, at the same time employing elements of that narrative to "reform" the system.

The story of *A Test of Leadership* is woven through a tapestry that pulls together several key elements of the progressive narrative. Its warp is the idea that America is progressing toward the achievement of a virtuous democracy; the weft is a story about how American higher education has failed to appropriately recast this narrative for the twenty-first century and has thus fallen into declension from the promise embedded in it.

The opening of *Test of Leadership* invokes one of America's most familiar archetypes, the frontier, to root the document in the familiar context of American history and the American jeremiad (cf. Kolodny 1975; Slotkin 1985). In the first paragraph, the report argues that "higher education in the United States has become one of our greatest success stories." Colleges and universities, the report says, have helped to "advanc[e] the frontiers of knowledge," are "the envy of the world," and have "educated more people to higher levels than any other nation" (Miller 2006, vi). But American higher education has fallen away from this superior position, it says. From the viewpoint of the idea that the educational system has an obligation enable America's students to become participants in the democracy of opportunity, it is failing. "[A] lot of other countries have followed our lead," it claims, "and *they are educating more of their citizens to more advanced levels than we are* (vii, emphasis in original). This is problematic because "postsecondary instruction is increasingly vital to the nation's economic security[, y]et too many Americans just aren't getting the education that they need—and that they deserve" (vii).

The point made in the report's preface is reiterated throughout: threats to achievement of the promise—and the betrayal of education's fundamental mission—come from inside. High schools don't see "preparing all pupils for postsecondary education and training as their responsibility"; a "troubling number" of students who go on to college "waste time—and taxpayer dollars—mastering English and math skills that they should have learned in high school" (Miller 2006, vii). Colleges and universities "don't accept responsibility for making sure that those they admit actually do succeed," and there "is a lack of clear, reliable information about the cost and quality of postsecondary institutions, along with a remarkable absence of accountability mechanisms to ensure that colleges succeed in educating students" (vii). Institutions, it says, need to "do a better job . . . of teaching [students] what they need to learn" (vii). The "new landscape," it claims, "demands innovation and flexibility" because "[students] care—as we do—about results" (viii).

Following the establishment of this internal declension, two paragraphs in *A Test of Leadership* signal the application of principles emanating from the progressive pragmatic jeremiad. The first anchors the report squarely in the jeremiad's narrative:

> To reach these objectives, we believe that U.S. higher education institutions must recommit themselves to their core public purposes. For close to a century now, access to higher education has been a principle—some would say *the* principle—means of achieving social mobility. Much of our nation's inventiveness has been centered in colleges and universities, as has our commitment to a kind of democracy that only an educated and informed citizenry makes possible. It is not surprising that American institutions of higher education have become a magnet for attracting people of talent and ambition from throughout the world. (ix)

The code words here—core public purposes, access to higher education, achieve[ment] of social mobility, commitment to . . . democracy, educated and informed citizenry—all emphasize that achievement of a virtuous democracy relies upon the development of critical intelligence through education.

But the paragraph immediately following represents a pivotal moment in the report. It indicates that the educational system itself has fallen into declension and poses an obstacle to the achievement of the democracy at the jeremiad's end. Additionally, it intimates that educators, experts charged with the authority to direct this cultivation, no longer understand the nature of the virtuous democracy.

> But today that world is becoming tougher, more competitive, less forgiving of wasted resources and squandered opportunities. In tomorrow's world a nation's wealth will derive from its capacity to educate, attract, and retain citizens who are able to work smarter and learn faster—making educational achievement ever more important both for individuals and society writ large. (ix)

Today, this paragraph says, the world is different. For American students to achieve twenty-first-century democracy, steps toward that goal must be recast. Both of these paragraphs, then, represent versions of the progressive pragmatic narrative: both emphasize the crucial nature of the development of individual creative intelligence to the pursuit of the virtuous democracy, and both frame education as the means by which that end is achieved. The consequences of allegiance to the "old" ways are made clear—it will pull the democracy into declension. In fact, the report relies upon a vision of Progressive Era industry to make the point: "History is littered with industries that, at their peril, failed to respond to . . . changes in the world around them, from railroads to steel manufacturers" (ix). Then, in a masterful demonstration of the power of language, *A Test of Leadership* forges an iron frame around its argument. "Already," it claims, "troubling signs are abundant" (ix), and turns to reports about the United States' "ranking among major industrialized countries in higher education attainment" (ix). While it's possible to make a case that educational success could or should be defined differently, it becomes increasingly difficult in the tidal wave of economic and achievement data included in *Test of Leadership* to advance the case.[1]

Following this preamble, *Test of Leadership* continues to invoke the progressive pragmatic jeremiad to extend its analysis. "Colleges and universities," it says, "must continue to be the major route for new generations of Americans to achieve social mobility. And for the country as a whole, future economic growth will depend on our ability to sustain excellence, innovation, and leadership in higher education" (1). The "transformation of the world economy increasingly demands a more highly educated workforce with postsecondary skills and credentials," the report explains, and *that* is where the current system of higher education has begun to falter (6). The report goes on to outline areas in which these problems are most evident: access, alignment, affordability, and accountability (also known as the four "A"s). The problems begin before students enter college, when they encounter a financial aid system that is referred to in different places in the report as "confusing, complex, inefficient, duplicative" (3), "a maze" (3), and "dysfunctional" (9). Once admitted, students encounter an "alignment gap" between what they learn in high school and what is expected in college:

> High school faculty and administrators are unaware of the standards and assessments being used by their counterparts in the other sector. . . . Consequences of substandard prep and poor alignment between high schools and colleges persist in college. Remediation has become far too common an experience for American postsecondary students. Some 40 percent of all college students end up taking at least one remedial course—at an estimated cost to the taxpayers of $1 billion. (8)

The problems don't stop in college, though: "additionally, industry spends significant financial aid resources on remediation and retraining" (8). The "product," the report says, "is increasingly expensive, but not necessarily value-added" (2). It explains, later, that the results violate postsecondary education's commitment to mobility, and that postsecondary institutions (along with "national and state politicians") have perpetuated this denial because they refuse to make adjustments to their ossified structures:

According to the most recent National Assessment of Adult Literacy . . . the percentage of college graduates deemed proficient in prose literacy has actually declined from 40 to 31 percent in the past decade. These shortcomings have real-world consequences. Employers report repeatedly that many new graduates they hire are not prepared to work, lacking the critical thinking, writing and problem-solving skills needed in today's workplaces. In addition, business and government leaders have repeatedly and urgently called for workers at all stages of life to continually upgrade their academic and practical skills. But both national and state politicians and the practices of postsecondary institutions have not always made this easy, by failing to provide financial and logistical support for lifelong learning and by failing to craft flexible credit-transfer systems that allow students to move easily between different kinds of institutions. (3–4)

Further, postsecondary education reneges on its commitment to mobility because it does not provide an assessment of the effectiveness of its product. The "large and complex public-private system of federal, state, and private regulators has significant shortcomings," the report says. "Accreditation reviews are typically kept private, and those that are made public still focus on process reviews more than bottom-line results for learning or costs" (14). What is necessary, instead, is a system that is

more transparent about cost, price, and student success outcomes. Student achievement, which is inextricably connected to institutional success, must be measured by institutions on a "value added" basis that takes into account students' academic baseline when assessing their results. This information should be made available to students, and reported publicly in aggregate form to provide consumers and policymakers an accessible, understandable way to measure the relative effectiveness of different colleges and universities. (4)

Although the report claims that "we recognize that some who care deeply about higher education—and whose partnership we value in the new endeavors we propose—may not easily accept either our diagnosis or our prescriptions" (x), the challenges laid out in the report are clear.

As a case study of a report that might outline future policy, *A Test of Leadership* captures the formidable challenge facing contemporary educators. Employing a revision of Lippmann's technocratic contention that the sheer variety of symbols available to Americans will result in too many diverse interpretations and that this diversity will lead to failure to come to consensus around the appropriate interpretation, it suggests that educators have no sense of the direction of America's progress and cannot come to agreement even about what the virtuous democracy looks like. Lacking this big picture, strategic vision, they are unable to develop educational processes through which students can develop the critical intelligence necessary to participate in this democracy. This lack of understanding leads to the development of multiple, nonaligned processes. To straighten out the situation, then, it suggests that intervention from outside experts who have this vision and can develop an aligned curriculum around it is necessary.

READY AND WILLING: EXPERTS IN THE WINGS

The recommendations in *A Test of Leadership*—especially those connected to alignment and accountability—reflect what NCTE higher education policy liaison Paul Bodmer refers to as "the beltway consensus" about higher education. That is, the report distills a sense circulating in higher education policy circles that higher education is going its own way, ignorant of the (new) shape of the virtuous democracy, and not deliberately preparing students for participation in it (Bodmer 2007). This consensus reflects and has been perpetuated by a dizzying array of organizations and groups positioning themselves as possessing the kind of expertise required to reshape learning, cognizant both of the new version of democracy at the end of the jeremiad and of the means required to help the nation achieve that democracy.

Among the most influential of these organizations is Achieve, Inc. (which incorporates an element of the jeremiad in its very name). Created as a partnership with the National Association of Governors and business leaders, Achieve says that it "helps states raise academic standards and achievement so that all students graduate ready for college, work, and citizenship" (Achieve.org). Achieve, Inc., parent organization of Achieve. org, is also one of three partners—the Education Trust and the Thomas B. Fordham Foundation are the other two—in the American Diploma Project (ADP); ADP is one of the most influential outside groups attempting to assert their expertise in discussions about education by actively pressing for national alignment of secondary content and outcomes. Currently, ADP is working to reshape secondary curriculum in 30 states (Achieve.org). Because ADP is also pressing for alignment between high school outcomes and college expectations, their recommendations also de facto extend to postsecondary education as well.

ADP's recommendations are contained in another report, this one called *Ready or Not: Creating a High School Diploma That Counts*. Like the Spellings Report, this document also opens by explaining that educators no longer understand the shape of the virtuous democracy at the end of the jeremiad:

> For too many graduates, the American high school diploma signifies only a broken promise. While students and their parents may still believe that the diploma reflects adequate preparation for the intellectual demands of adult life, in reality it falls far short of this common sense goal. . . . The diploma has lost its value because what it takes to earn one is disconnected from what it takes for graduates to compete successfully beyond high school. . . . (ADP 1)

Ready or Not goes on to explain that "experts" (in English and mathematics, the specific foci of ADP's efforts) do not understand "real-world demands" and therefore craft curriculum that reflects "what is desirable for students to learn, but not necessarily what is essential for them to be prepared for further learning, work or citizenship after completing high school" (ADP 7–8).

Ready or Not then suggests that, to restore the nation's course, it is necessary for students to understand and be educated for participation in a different kind of democracy, one that is driven by the "require[ments] . . . of employees and students" (21). Although postsecondary educators are included as part of the group who should establish those requirements, they also are mentioned as some "experts" crafting curriculum around what is "desirable," but not "essential." Thus it is primarily employers whose requirements must be met to propel the nation forward—but not just any employers. ADP looks specifically to a narrow range of "fast-growing occupations . . . identified in the ADP workplace study," including "plant, production and construction managers, marketing and events managers, engineers and engineering technicians, . . . medical professionals and health technicians, . . . foresters, . . . computer programmers and IT workers, . . . and teachers" (23). The report suggests that to move the nation toward the achievement of democracy, students (employees) must be trained to meet the needs of these workplaces.

Because, *Ready or Not* says, secondary and postsecondary teachers neither understand nor are educating students for these professions, ADP is ready to step in. The report offers a set of benchmarks and curricular frameworks that are based on interactions with postsecondary faculty and business leaders that will fill the need identified by ADP. These include prescriptive (and narrowly constructed) reading lists (of the 47 texts listed under "Fiction: Classic and Contemporary," for example, the newest is Gish Jen's *Typical American*; only 15 are written by women; and only 12 by nonwhite authors) and sample tasks like writing letters requesting fiduciary credit or inviting people to participate in panel presentations (38–40, 83–85).

FRAMING AND METHODOLOGY: ADP AND BEYOND

The methodology used for the conversations that resulted in ADP's lists and sample tasks also indicate just how powerful the frame surrounding current discussions of education—especially the influence of outside expertise—is. For the ADP's postsecondary meetings, representatives examined a number of tests—"high school graduation tests, national college admissions and placement tests, a sampling of post-secondary tests; and the GED"—"to codify what the *de facto* standards are for students by evaluating the content of the various assessments they are asked to take" (ADP 107). This methodology necessarily assumes that these exams also correctly incorporate and represent the critical intelligence that educators seek to develop in high school and college.

Of course, this assumption is enormously complicated. The pressures on educators—from NCLB, budget cuts, and schools and districts—have never been greater. One consequence of these pressures has been for institutions to turn toward standardized assessments such as the ones described by ADP. At the same time, however, many teachers also recognize that these tests are highly flawed and do not in fact represent what they would like to teach or have their students learn—see, for instance, the testimonials included on sites like educational critic Susan Ohanian's Web site (Ohanian). ADP—and maybe even the teachers gathered by ADP—may assume that teachers endorse the "*de facto* standards" that they presume these tests represent, but the teachers writing to Ohanian's site—along with research by educators like Alfie Kohn, Denny Taylor, Richard Allington, and many others—makes a very different case. These tests are used because they are expedient, they are relatively inexpensive for districts to administer, and they *are* widely used.

Developers of many of these tests also assert that their instruments—that is, the tests themselves—are among the methods and devices that are critical for propelling the nation forward toward the achievement of the virtuous democracy. In a letter included in ACT's 2006 annual report, for instance, CEO Richard Ferguson suggests that ACT has and will continue to develop products that teachers can use to achieve the new shape of the virtuous democracy. He writes that there is now growing concern . . . that, in general, the courses offered in the nation's high schools are not sufficiently rigorous. . . .

To help address this challenging reality, we will soon be launching *QualityCore*™, an assessment system based on a new model for raising the rigor of high school courses. *QualityCore* is intended both to increase student achievement in core courses and to improve the effectiveness of curriculum, instruction, and assessment in these courses. . . . (Ferguson 2006, 3)

As a major marketer of tests and curriculums, ACT also asserts that it regularly seeks input from stakeholders, including educators, to design the tests and curriculum that they market. This is the purpose, for instance, of the ACT National Curriculum Survey (NCS), administered to high school and college instructors on a regular basis. That survey provides the evidence for an assertion made by ACT in a press release following data analysis of the study (and repeated in news stories around the country in publications from *USA Today* to the *Daily Oklahoman*): that there is a gap between what students learn in high school and what college instructors expect; that "colleges generally want all incoming students to attain in-depth understanding of a selected number of fundamental skills and knowledge in their high school courses, while high schools tend to provide less in-depth instruction of a broader range of skills and topics" (ACT 2007b; Markelein 2007; Simpson 2007).

But an analysis of the most recent version of this survey, administered in 2005–2006, reveals that it is also highly problematic.[2] The NCS purports to address broad questions about college readiness, but it primarily seems intended to inform the development and marketing of the Educational Planning and Assessment System (EPAS), which includes EXPLORE (administered in sixth grade), PLAN (administered in tenth grade), ACT (their college entrance exam), WorkKeys (a work preparation assessment), and curricular products designed to support the development of skills assessed by the exams. An analysis of the survey results in the report appendix suggests that the survey questionnaire itself contains questions framed by ACT's understanding of writing skills as associated with "readiness," rather than a frame that might make it possible for respondents to contribute their own ideas about a concept.[3]

The NCS report also seems to overgeneralize the survey's results based on an ill-defined sample of respondents (e.g., Rea and Parker 1992, 118–31). It asserts that its claims are based on a "nationally representative" sample (ACT 2007a 2, 3), but no information is provided in it about what makes the sample receiving or responding to it "representative." A graphic included in appendix A breaks down the surveys sent by subject matter. 1,600 "English/Writing" surveys were distributed to middle/junior high school teachers of "English/Language Arts"; 2,000 to high school teachers of "Writing/Composition"; 1,097 to entry-level college course instructors of "Composition"; 403 to entry-level college teachers of "Freshman English," and 800 to entry-level instructors of "Survey of American Literature." An additional 1,246 surveys were sent to "Developmental Writing" instructors (ACT 2007a, 36). But the report includes no definitions of these courses (e.g., it does not define the difference between "Composition" and "Freshman English") or a description of the faculty to whom these surveys were sent (e.g., whether they were sent to full-time lecturers, faculty, or part-time instructors; what training these respondents had with regard to the subjects that they were teaching; and so on). And although these different areas of "English" are broken out in a description of survey *recipients*, the same breakouts do not appear in the information about survey *respondents*. Table A.2 of appendix A, "English/Writing Survey Response Rate," indicates the number of surveys returned by middle/junior high teachers, high school teachers, postsecondary instructors, and "remedial course" instructors. Additionally, the response rates among these groups were quite low—not more than 18 percent (or 363 of 2,000 distributed) of the surveys distributed to any group were returned (this highest percentage coming from high school teachers) (ACT 2007a, 36). Thus any assertion that the ACT (or any other part of the EPAS) is representative of a valid or reliable survey of instructors of writing (or any of the other delineations identified within the survey) is circumspect at best, and certainly must be placed within the broader context of ACT's interests.[4]

Despite these methodological issues, ACT has used the results of the NCS to construct a narrative that reflects the same use of the progressive pragmatic jeremiad in documents like *A Test of Leadership* and *Ready or Not*. This story has been circulated in a press release from ACT and repeated (sometimes verbatim) in other news stories as evidence of the inference that teachers and the educational system do not understand the nature of twenty-first-century democracy, that they are not preparing students to participate in it, and that outside intervention (in the form of the ACT EPAS) is required to restore the educational system to its rightful course. ACT then proposes a solution to this problem: use of its own expertise. This solution is outlined in ACT's marketing materials (the NCS report, ACT's annual report, and so on). In the letter included in the 2006 annual report, for instance, CEO Ferguson notes that ACT is

> also committed to supporting educators and policymakers as they work to enhance the quality of high school courses and remove barriers to student achievement, state by state. With support through the National Governors Association [NGA] Center for Best Practices grants, three states . . . are now working with ACT and the NGA on a pilot project designed to improve the rigor of high school courses. The project includes professional development workshops for teachers and administrators to evaluate course quality and improve instruction. . . . (Ferguson 2006, 3–4)

Perhaps not surprisingly, ACT cites research by the Thomas B. Fordham Foundation (one of the three partners in the ADP) to support their claim that high school teachers are asked to teach too many things (NCS Report, 5); as above, Ferguson's letter notes that the organization is working with educators in Oklahoma, Mississippi, and Pennsylvania—all ADP states—on a pilot project (ACT annual report 4). ACT tests (including the

ACT and WorkKeys exams) are also administered to all high school juniors in six states (ACT annual report 4).

WEAVING AN ALTERNATIVE: NCTE AND COVERAGE OF THE SAT WRITING EXAM

As this analysis of *A Test of Leadership, Ready or Not*, and the ACT NCS illustrates, a technocratic, interventionist version of the pragmatic progressive jeremiad can support a frame in which stories suggest that educators have lost their ability to outline a process (or a related set of processes) for students to develop the critical intelligence necessary to participate in twenty-first-century democracy. This frame also justifies intervention from outside experts—ADP, ACT, and others—to offer alternative means for moving the nation toward the achievement of this democracy. But the progressive pragmatic jeremiad also contains the possibility for alternative frames as well; these frames contain other possibilities for action.

An analysis of the NCTE's actions surrounding coverage of the rolling out of the SAT writing exam in 2005 illustrates how strategies and narratives that are also rooted in this jeremiad can be used to construct alternative frames for stories about teachers and education.[5] Initially, news coverage of this new exam reflected the same narratives as those in reports like those discussed earlier. That is, they were framed by a narrative that schools are not adequately preparing students for this life; students' writing abilities, especially, are in decline; educational institutions (teachers, students) have not been able to stop the slide; outside agents (such as the College Board) can provide necessary leverage (in the best case scenario) or interventions (in the worst) to restore students' abilities and, therefore, ensure that they are developing (writing) skills necessary for their success as future citizens. This argument is evident, for instance, in a *New York Times Magazine* feature story, "Writing to the Test":

> Changes like the new writing test amount to a kind of arm-twisting. The College Board is adding an essay in part to force schools to

pay more attention to the teaching of writing, which Mr. [Gaston] Caperton [head of the College Board and the former governor of West Virginia] believes is being shamefully neglected. He's not the only one who thinks so. In 2003, the National Commission on Writing in America's Schools and Colleges, a study group convened by the College Board, discovered, among other things, that most fourth-grade students spend less than three hours a week writing, or a fraction of the time they spend watching television; that nearly two-thirds of high school seniors do not write a three-page paper as often as once a month for their English classes; and that the long research paper has pretty much become a thing of the past. One result is that by the time they get to college, more than 50 percent of incoming freshmen are unable to produce papers relatively free of language errors and to analyze arguments or synthesize information. (McGrath 2004)

In a separate story, Caperton argued that this new exam would "create a revolution in the schools" because including it in the SAT would require teachers to attend to writing in the classroom (quoted in Franek 2005).

Early news coverage after the exam's first administration continued to perpetuate these stories. They reported that the exam was aligned with what was taught in high school and students would do well on the test because of that reflection (Holmes 2005; Roebuck 2005; Kollali 2005); that the exam would create a stronger entering class because it reinforced what students learned in high school (Holmes 2005; Woods 2005; Roebuck 2005; Kollali 2005; Feldmeier 2005); and that the exam also reflected what students would learn in college (Holmes 2005; Stephens 2005; Kollali 2005).

But on May 4, 2005, two stories appeared that precipitated a significant shift in the coverage of the SAT writing exam: one in the *Washington Post* and one in the *New York Times*. The lead in the *Post* story illustrates this shift:

A professional organization representing 60,000 teachers of English criticized the new essay portion of the SAT as a poor predictor of

> how well students will perform in college and expressed concern
> that it could encourage mediocre, formulaic writing.
>
> The report by the National Council of Teachers of English
> comes as half a million students prepare to take the SAT this
> weekend. . . .
>
> The skills that are needed to do well on this test represent a very
> narrow range of the skills that students will need to do well in the
> marketplace," said Robert Yagelski, a professor of English education
> at the State University of New York at Albany and chairman of the
> task force that drew up the report. (Dobbs 2005)

This lead reflects a different story, one that is rooted in a different version of the progressive pragmatic narrative. Here the lead makes the case that the College Board and the SAT, not teachers, do not understand the nature of twenty-first-century democracy and that the exam (as one method by which students' critical intelligence might be cultivated or demonstrated) will not contribute to what students need to have for success. The narratives appearing in the Washington Post story—that the new SAT writing exam would encourage formulaic writing used only in testing situations, that it was a poor predictor of success, and that it might lead to a narrowing of writing instruction—were also repeated in a New York Times news item about an analysis of the correlation between exam length and exam score conducted by MIT faculty member Les Perelman. The first paragraph of the Times story repeats the claim in the Post that the exam is developing "poor" writing skills, then quotes Perelman as an expert to identify the problem. "'It appeared to me that regardless of what a student wrote, the longer the essay, the higher the score,' Dr. Perelman said. . . . In the next weeks, Dr. Perelman studied every graded sample SAT that the College Board made public. . . . He was stunned by how complete the correlation was between length and score" (Winerip 2005). These two stories signaled a significant shift. Between March 13 and May 4, 27 of 29 articles (included in a content analysis) were framed by the technocratic, interventionist narrative described earlier. After their publication, 15 stories published about the SAT writing exam between May 5 and August 15 (in the same analysis) were dominated by the frame represented in the *Post* and *Times* stories (Adler-Kassner, "Framing").

Even in 2007, the SAT writing exam is often covered as controversial. A story in the *Pittsburgh Post-Gazette*, for example, noted that "the National Council of Teachers of English two years ago said the writing test was 'unlikely to improve college writing instruction,'" and included a quote from then-President-Elect Kathleen Blake Yancey of NCTE about the exam (Chute 2007). Another story in the *Record* (Bergen County, New Jersey) cited a "wait and see approach [to the SAT exam that] seems prevalent among a generation of admissions officers who have expressed growing dissatisfaction with the SAT" (Alex 2007). Following Les Perelman's presentation at the 2007 Conference on College Composition and Communication (CCCC), where he reported the results of an experiment to game the SAT by training a subject (over 18 and with consent) to produce a lengthy but error-riddled essay that then received the highest possible score from SAT raters, coverage of the SAT that reflected perspectives advanced by NCTE was back in the news. A story in *Inside Higher Education* appeared only days after Perleman's presentation; shortly afterward it was circulating among blogs and listservs and had appeared on University Wire, a news service for college and university newspapers. And while many colleges and universities continue to use the SAT and the writing exam, over 350 colleges have made the SAT optional for admission. While some of these institutions did not require the exam before this controversy, a number have made the decision since (e.g., College of the Holy Cross, Mount Holyoke, and Spellman) (Glod and Matthews 2006; FairTest).

STRATEGIES FOR SUCCESS: NCTE AND FRAMING THE SAT WRITING EXAM STORY

This shift in frames around coverage of the NCTE writing exam did not happen accidentally. To help effect it, NCTE drew on strategies that also seem to draw (at least in part) from the pragmatic progressive jeremiad. Ultimately, these strategies resulted in three clear messages: "That good writing instruction as described in *NCTE Beliefs about the Teaching of Writing* is the best preparation for success in writing; that the test may take away from good writing instruction; and about the test as a test of writing and the issues of validity, equity, and other uses" (Davis 2005, 3). But NCTE worked through a dialogic, methodical process designed to gather input from and build on the critical intelligences of their membership in order to craft this message in such a way as to represent the interests of that group. This process was enacted through NCTE's strategic governance model. Through it, NCTE regularly surveys its membership, asking what Executive Director Kent Williamson describes as two simple questions: "What do you see as the most influential issues shaping your professional practice in the year ahead?" and "What is most essential to you?" (Williamson 1996). These open-ended questions are quite different than the directive ones sent to an ambiguously identified sample receiving the ACT National Curriculum Survey; they are also circulated to an identified group of NCTE's membership. They represent an effort on NCTE's behalf to work systematically, methodically, and through a process to gather input that can be used to contribute to (and shape) the creative intelligence of NCTE members.

This process also continues beyond the survey. Results are relayed to the elected NCTE presidential team, who then identifies between one and three issues of focus for the following year. Next the organization (and its members) identify trends likely to influence those issues in the next three to five years and surveys the resources available on these issues within the organization (e.g., research, position statements, etc.). NCTE then explores what possible partnerships might be forced to "fill in gaps" or proceed to action on identified issues. Finally the organization investigates the "ethical dimensions" of its choices—what they might mean for others and what the consequences of taking a particular action might be for members and students (Williamson 1996).

Two of the issues identified in the 2004 survey of members tied into concerns with the new SAT writing exam (Davis 2005).

Additionally, NCTE leadership drew on the existing *Framing Statements on Assessment* and created the *NCTE Beliefs about the Teaching of Writing*, both of which represented best practice (research and experience) in the field and reflected input from members. Following these actions, NCTE President Randy Bomer convened a task force of members to study the SAT and ACT writing exams. That group agreed to focus their work on four areas of research related to the exams: validity and reliability; the "unintended use" of the exams; "the impact of the tests on curriculum and classroom instruction;" and "the impact of the tests on attitudes toward writing and writing instruction" (Davis 2005). They then engaged in another systematic, methodical process of research, collaboration, and drafting that took into account the interests and ideals of NCTE members (as represented in professional documents and discussions) to craft a report that served as the basis for NCTE's framing of the SAT and ACT writing exams.

As a case study, then, NCTE's work on reframing coverage of these writing exams offers some useful lessons. First, reframing doesn't happen quickly, and it doesn't just happen in published news stories. Instead it starts by laying groundwork that involves discovering and identifying principles and considering how those principles extend to specific elements of practice, among the key strategies described more fully in chapter 4. In this case, NCTE's strategic governance model helped to lay the groundwork that underscored the task force's work, and therefore the position adopted by NCTE.

Second, it involves working with and involving lots of people, not just the position of one person (or of a small group). Again, NCTE's strategic governance model is important here—the *NCTE Beliefs on the Teaching of Writing* that are reflected in the task force's positions were developed before this report was written—and not necessarily as a response to a particular threat to those beliefs, but as a foundation for the organization's work.

The beliefs of that group then serve as a basis from which to develop alliances with other individuals and groups who hold related positions and who can also support the frame-changing—in this case, NCTE reached out to the National Writing Project, FairTest, and even to the College Board (who received an embargoed draft of NCTE's report before it appeared). Fourth, frame-changing work is focused. NCTE identified three positions that they would take with regard to this exam. They then trained spokespeople, who advanced these positions both as responses to specific questions and as hooks for compelling news stories. NCTE also released the report strategically—first in InBox ("so that we could make our own news with our own news vehicle," according to Davis [2005, 2]), then to previously made contacts at major newspapers, National Public Radio (NPR), and smaller news media (3). These strategies, too, are important parts of the story-changing strategic work described in chapter 4.

PROFESSIONAL POSITIONING: PUBLIC/ACTIVIST INTELLECTUALISM

NCTE's work shifting frames around the SAT writing exam raises one final question that is embedded in Joseph Harris's oft-quoted statement about compositionists' "inability" to effectively express our positions among wider audiences: how should we position ourselves and our work with regard to our constituents, our potential allies, and the broader issues that are addressed in and through our work? As Peter Mortensen asserted in "Going Public," this issue should be at the core of what we do:

> In our journals and at our conferences, one finds repeated again and again the assertion that our work—our teaching, researching, and theorizing—can clarify and even improve the prospects of literacy in democratic culture. If we really believe this, we must then acknowledge our obligation to air that work in the most expansive, inclusive forums imaginable. (182)

Christian Weisser offers two possible roles for academics to occupy in these "expansive, inclusive forums." One is what Weisser calls the "public intellectual," defined by Stanley Fish as "someone who takes as his or her subject matters of public concern and has the public's attention" (quoted in Weisser 2002, 118). This public intellectual plays a central role in the progressive pragmatic jeremiad, of course. She is the person who connects the values of the broader culture to the classroom and cultivates students' critical intelligences so that they can do the same, either through cultivation or imposition. But as Ellen Cushman notes, this conception of teaching is shot through with a paternalism that also is included in pragmatic progressivism. Cushman points to an example from Michael Berube's work to illustrate the point. Berube writes that

> the future of our ability to produce new knowledges for and about ordinary people—and the availability of education to ordinary people—may well depend on how effectively [academics] can . . . make our work intelligible to nonacademics—who then, we hope, will be able to recognize far-right rant about academe for what it is. (quoted in Cushman 1999, 329)

In this conception, "we" produce knowledge for and about ordinary people. This conception of academic work echoes David J. Rothman's description of progressives, whom he says were:

> so attached to a paternalistic model that they never considered the potential of their programs to be as coercive as they were liberating. In their eagerness to play parent to the child, they did not pause to ask whether the dependent had to be protected against their [Progressives'] own well-meaning interventions. (72)

"Public intellectualism" also lies at the base of what Eli Goldblatt calls the "throughput model," the idea that students move through the university "with the occasional field trip or lab to indicate that the learning they do has application in a world outside of school" (Goldblatt 2005, 276). Paula Mathieu argues that this notion of the academic also underscores seeing community-university partnerships as "strategic"—controlled by the university and ultimately furthering its interests, rather than those of the community. The "academic as public intellectual" also underscores the "charity-oriented" service-learning models described in chapter 2 of this book (Mathieu 2005).

The other potential role available to academics, Weisser suggests, is that of an "activist intellectual," one who strives to build connections between her intellectual work and specific work in specific sites among particular audiences (Weisser 2002, 118). Mathieu refers to this work as "tactical" because it is site, time, and project-specific and is grounded in the interests of the partnering organization and the collaborating instructor, rather than the long-term interests of the institution (Mathieu 2005, xiv). Goldblatt draws on the work of Saul Alinsky to make a case for this model, one of "long-term investment in the neighborhoods where we work and centers with which we form partnerships . . . a model of community-based learning and research in which students and their teachers are not so much providing services as participating in a collective effort defined by academics and local citizens alike" (Goldblatt 2005, 283). The idea of activist intellectualism is at the core of efforts like those described by Cushman, Goldblatt, Linda Flower and her colleagues at the Pittsburgh Literacy Center, and others who focus on developing long-term relationships that reflect the interests of community *and* campus, and where university partners "show a consistent presence in the community and an investment in creating knowledge with and for community members" (Cushman 2002, 58). This model takes into consideration the issues of context, material culture, and everyday living, working, and other conditions that are not explicitly included in the conception of progressive pragmatism that has often fueled the educational project.

Acting as activist intellectuals—that is, enacting a more carefully articulated, materially based notion of progressive pragmatism—is also crucial if educators (including WPAs and writing instructors) are to shift the frames surrounding documents like A *Test of Leadership, Ready or Not,* and other that assert the authority of "experts" over educators. This activism can begin with critique as a necessary part of the application of critical intelligence, but then it must build upon that critique to develop, with interested stakeholders, a different narrative that reflects the interests and passions of those involved. It is possible, for instance, that Brian Huot's critique of the Spellings Report, published in the May 2007 *College English*, is the kind of response that is now required. But that piece (and others) will serve as this kind of foundation only if their critiques are one of many elements included in a story-changing process. The problem, communication theorist James Carey asserts, is that the technocratic mode of progressivism discussed in the previous chapter has reduced "the public . . . to a phantom" and "citizens . . . [to] objects rather than the subjects of politics" (Carey 1997a, 247). That is, if all educators do is critique, we position ourselves as agents who can only refute analyses that lead to this "reduction," not as ones who can also take actions reflecting our interests and those of others.

In this sense, activist intellectualism requires engaging in the dialectical, dialogic process that is a central component of progressive pragmatism, updated to the twenty-first century. Through this dialectic, individuals and groups bring their own cultures and experiences to the development of methods for developing critical intelligence; the cultures, experiences, and values reflected in these methods is then *also* analyzed and critiqued so that it is as representative *of* those cultures and experiences (and not just of the individuals who have contributed to them) as possible. The construction of knowledge is a collective, not an individual, activity; the development of tropes, narratives, code words, and frames emanating from those tropes also becomes a collaborative activity. The question becomes not whose views are represented, but what roles might be available for people to play within these processes of construction and dissemination. This perspective, then, stands in direct opposition to the logical evolution of technocratic, interventionist instantiations of the progressive pragmatic jeremiad, where individuals are dragged along within frames because those frames echo a kind of groupthink created for and spoon-fed to the populous by experts. At the same time, however, it also augments the humanitarian, stewardly conception of that jeremiad, attempting to address the issues of paternalism embedded in its evasion of materiality by explicitly taking into consideration issues of power, context, and culture not originally included in the narrative extending from it.

Through this revision of the progressive pragmatic model, reframing becomes more than just an attempt to, say, shift the focus of coverage of a news subject—for example, students in college-level writing courses or the work that is completed in those courses. In fact, it is an attempt to create a different kind of public sphere, a republican (small "r") one requiring "often cacophonous conversation" (Carey 1997b, 219). These models for intellectual work, like the models for action based on that work presented by the NCTE's success with reframing coverage of the SAT writing exam, rest on making connections between what compositionists (and WPAs) value, what is important to us in and about our work, and then proceeding from that point to build alliances with others that provide benefits for us and for them. These points are reiterated by the community organizers whose work is used as the basis for developing strategies for WPAs and writing instructors to use in our reframing work described in the next two chapters.

4

CHANGING CONVERSATIONS ABOUT WRITING AND WRITERS
Working through a Process

Justine, a tenured WPA at a small, religiously affiliated university, has a dilemma.[1]

> At the last minute the chair decides to move a faculty member from first-year composition to a course in the major. As WPA I have to scurry and find a replacement instructor. The dean won't allow either of the two single course adjuncts that we have to teach another section because it will make them "full time" so I have to hire someone new on short notice. Our pay falls in the middle range of the many colleges in the area—higher than most state schools but lower than the other private schools that are more of our peer institutions. But because this is already late December, it is hard to find people whose schedule can accommodate the course.
>
> After interviewing two people the more experienced, more qualified person turns it down because of the pay. What should I do? Hire the second choice, someone who has only one semester of teaching first-year composition at community colleges with very different curriculum, student population, etc.? What if I decide not to hire anyone and just say we don't have any qualified people available? How can I get the chair—and the dean—to understand that we need more than a warm body . . . and that all of our students— who pay $30,000 a year for tuition—deserve more and in fact need highly qualified instructors?

CHANGING STORIES: STRATEGIES WITH IDEALS

Justine's story encompasses some of the field's most pressing challenges, all of which extend from the stories about writing and writers discussed in chapters 2 and 3. How are students' literacies defined when they come in to composition courses? What should courses teach to develop students' literacies—or, in the language of the progressive pragmatic jeremiad, to cultivate students' critical intelligences—and for what purposes? Finally, how should students' literacies (or critical intelligences) be assessed at the ends of these courses?

Institutional responses to these questions extend to some of the most critical issues identified in WPA research in the last 20 years. These include the role of WPAs' work within the institution (how is it defined? valued? rewarded? [e.g., Bloom; Huot; Micciche 2002]); the relationships that exist between WPAs and other instructors teaching writing courses (are they equals? who has more authority? why? how is this authority extended? [e.g., Desmet 2005; Hesse 1999]); and, of course, hiring and staffing practices (who should be hired, at what salary, with what benefits, why, and how? [e.g., Schell 1998; Hansen; Miller and Cripps 2005; Bosquet 2004; Harris 1997.) The short-term solution—hire the second choice—addresses Justine's immediate problem. But in choosing that option, she runs the risk of perpetuating narratives about the purposes and design of writing classes and programs that she might not want to, like "anyone can teach writing classes," or "writing instructors are a dime a dozen, so we don't need to pay them well." The long-term solution—not hiring anyone and instead taking up questions about who is qualified to teach, or what students deserve and why—may have other consequences for students in the (unstaffed) course or for Justine herself.

This chapter and the next one offer frameworks for WPAs to think about dilemmas like Justine's, as well as the many other kinds of dilemmas we face. Embedded in these frameworks is an argument that we can borrow strategies from people who are already engaged in the work of changing stories—not stories about writing per se, but other stories—and adapt them to our own needs. These frameworks and the strategies within them draw from interviews with and observations of community organizers and media activists as well as literature on organizing and change to identify processes and actions that are potentially useful for the purpose of affecting conversations about writing and writers. At each step, though, there are decisions to be made—about appropriate directions for work in our specific contexts, about the implications of decisions, about where to go and what to do next. If WPAs and writing instructors can use these strategies, maybe we won't face the kind of Faustian bargain that Justine will make here, a dilemma that both reflects and flows directly from the kind of frames reflected in big-picture policies analyzed in the previous chapters.

Other WPAs have suggested that ours is a position from which it is possible to affect what I am here referring to as story-changing work. Barbara Cambridge and Ben McClelland, for example, made the case over ten years ago that the WPA position affords the possibility to "orchestrate [a] broad strategic vision, develop [a] shared administrative and organizational infrastructure, and create the cultural glue which can create synergies" between writing programs and their institutions (Cambridge and McClelland 1995, 157). Lynn Bloom, similarly, outlined several areas where she believed that WPAs might have an effect in a relatively short period of time: training instructors, "influencing graduate . . . [and] undergraduate education," and shaping other faculty members' work with writing (Bloom 74). The strategies here build on the potential embedded in statements like Cambridge and McClelland's and Bloom's by situating them in the current context for discussions about writing (and education more generally), and by bringing to them a framework for potential change-making strategies.

This framework is drawn from the work of community organizers and media strategists who work for a number of organizations—MoveOn.org, Wellstone Action, the Industrial Areas Foundation (IAF), the Rockridge Institute, the SPIN Project, and others. Although these organizations address diverse concerns, they do so from ideologies that are considered progressive and left-leaning and from values that are certainly not dominant in the late stages of the Bush administration. While there are certainly right-leaning conservative organizations that also engage in frame-setting, their work seemed less salient for the purposes of this research. The success of the right's efforts to control terms of discussion about everything from foreign policy to education has been well documented in books like Thomas Frank's *What's the Matter with Kansas* and Geoffrey Nunberg's *Talking Right*; in films like Michael Moore's *Fahrenheit 911*; and almost nightly on shows like *The Daily Show* and *The Colbert Report*. Educators who want to change stories—WPAs, for instance, who might want to employ strategies to shift the frames around writing and writers on their own campuses—are often working against instantiations of this dominant narrative as it is represented in documents like *A Test of Leadership* (the final report of the Spellings Commission on Higher Education), *Ready or Not*, and the report on the ACT National Curriculum Survey discussed in chapter 3. Rather than look to expert sources whose strategies have been used to maintain and develop this dominant cultural narrative, it seemed more logical to look to ones who had achieved some measure of success in shifting this narrative in the ways that WPAs and writing instructors might want to do.

MEET THE INFORMANTS

The analysis in chapters 3 and 4 suggests that WPAs and writing instructors need to at least be cognizant of the ideologies associated with the frames currently shaping discussions about education (and writing), and perhaps work from different ideologies. Additionally, the Llewellyn quote invoked in chapter 1 attests to our need to learn how to change stories about writing and writers in systematic ways.

The very talented informants whose intelligence and ideas appear throughout this project, and from whose ideas I'll borrow to propose some possible strategies for story-changing work, include:

Joan Blades, a cofounder of MoveOn and of Moms Rising. With 3.3 million members (as of this writing),

MoveOn is an Internet-based organizing effort bringing together Americans who are interested in working for progressive social change. Hundreds of thousands of MoveOn members have mobilized to affect debate and action on issues from health care to voting. MoveOn was also the first organization to use the Internet as a mobilizing tool, creating online and offline forums for members to shape the direction of the organization. Moms Rising (www.momsrising.org), a new organization devoted to advocating for the rights of working mothers, was founded in May 2006.

Bruce Budner, executive director of the Rockridge Institute. Founded by linguist George Lakoff, Rockridge is a progressive policy institute that partners with allies to reshape the frames through which individuals and groups communicate their messages. In the last year, Rockridge has also become active in advocating for left-leaning frames, writing and distributing articles on important issues to blogs like the Huffington Post and Truthout. Rockridge's research demonstrates that their work on framing has affected the ways that targeted issues are discussed in mainstream media and online (Rockridge 2007).

Michel Gelobter, director of Redefining Progress, "the country's leading policy institute for smart economics, policies that help protect the environment and grow the economy, also known . . . as sustainability policy" (Gelobter 2006). Redefining Progress was founded in the mid-1990s as a "direction-setting institution" whose mission is to change the ways that Americans think about and work toward the future of the nation, using sustainability as a centerpiece for that thinking (and related action).

Eleanor Milroy, senior organizer for the Bay Area Organizing Committee, a project of the Chicago-based

Industrial Areas Foundation (IAF). Founded in 1940 by Saul Alinsky, the IAF is the nation's oldest established community organizing agency. IAF organizers work with local networks and individuals around the United States to identify issues for action. Among their successes are living wage ordinances (in New York, Texas, and Arizona); the development of affordable housing (in New York, Philadelphia, Baltimore, and Washington D.C.); and job creation programs (in Texas).

Erik Peterson, director of Labor Education Programs for Wellstone Action, an organization devoted to training grassroots leaders and activists. Founded in 2003 after the deaths of Paul and Sheila Wellstone, Wellstone Action's mission is to train and mobilize individuals and organizations. Wellstone Action sponsors over 70 "Camp Wellstones" each year, including special camps for college students where individuals can learn strategies for political campaigning and grassroots organizing. They also offer a number of specialized trainings to specific groups (e.g., labor unions, political candidates). Camp Wellstone graduates have been elected to school boards, state legislatures, and mayors' offices, and are involved in a number of grassroots organizing efforts. Peterson is also director of Northern Minnesota Programs for the Labor Education Service at the University of Minnesota.

Anat Shenker-Osorio, cofounder of Real Reason, an organization that "conducts long-term, cognitive research" to help organizations discover the values that underlie their existing or potential messages, develop strategies to implement messages that are in accordance with that message, and develop educational curricula on developing and aligning organizations around core principles. Before cofounding Real Reason, Shenker-Osorio was affiliated with the Rockridge Institute, where she and colleagues worked to develop and articulate the linguistic strategies that underscore that institute's work.

Laura Sapanora, communications strategist at the Strategic Press Information Network (SPIN) Project. SPIN helps other nonprofits develop communication strategies—developing communications plans, framing messages, developing skills to communicate with media organizations, and putting together a public profile.

IDENTIFYING STORIES/SETTING GOALS

What stories do we want to change? And how do we do it? Justine, for example, could talk to people already working in her writing program and listen, through their conversations, for issues that they felt were important, then try to work on those issues. Those issues might or might not include the issues that she raised in the vignette at the beginning of this chapter. Alternatively, Justine could try to rally people around values that she considers central to her own work and the work of her program, articulated in statements about "what students deserve" or "the foundational core of a good education." She also might try to organize people in her program and across campus around issues that she, as the WPA, has identified as important, like the qualifications of instructors teaching writing courses.

These three hypothetical approaches represent different approaches that stretch along a spectrum of organizing approaches. They also lead to different (but related) processes for organizing, processes that are also in some senses rooted in progressive pragmatism as it has evolved through the twentieth and twenty-first centuries. This chapter will describe each of the three approaches—interest-based organizing, values-based organizing, and issue-based organizing—and explore how they might be useful in our own context of writing instruction and administration.

For the sake of clarity I will separate them into three models; however, it is important to stress that they share points of intersection.
In fact, organizers employ elements of all of these strategies at different times. In her book about applying organizing practices to
K-12 teaching and advocacy, *Teachers Organizing for Change*, Cathy
Fleischer introduced the term in organizing literature used for
this blending: "mix[ing] and phas[ing]" (Fleischer 83).

Each of the approaches to story-changing work described
here begins from common assumptions. First, they assume
that story-changing work incorporates and proceeds from
principles—ones held by those participating in the organizing,
ones held by the organizer, or both. Identifying and articulating
principles, in fact, are essential for this work and serve as its very
core. Second, they assume that changing stories, even stories
like the ones in policy documents like *A Test of Leadership* or
news stories, must begin at the local level and is best done pro-
actively. Acting locally and ahead of "crisis," WPAs and writing
instructors can work in our own milieus, with our own people,
and work to steer the discussion. These three approaches also
share common goals: affecting change; developing a broad, self-
sustaining base of supporters; and using change to expand that
base. The tactics used in each approach vary slightly, however,
and also affect the ways that the first of those common goals—
affecting change—is defined. In interest-based organizing,
change is defined by and stems from the specific, short-term
interests of individuals who have come together to work for
that change. In values-based organizing, change is framed in
the long-term, strategic values held in common by a group.
Issue-based organizing, especially as it is discussed here, blends
interest- and values-approaches, working to achieve identified
interests that reflect individuals' short-term goals in the context
of long-term, strategic values.

TACTICS AND STRATEGIES

Conceptualizing these terms and understanding the
choices associated with *tactical* and *strategic* decisions are

important for writing instructors and WPAs who want to change stories, as they are for more experienced organizers.

Most discussions of tactics and strategies in academic literature draw on Michel deCerteau's *The Practice of Everyday Life*. There, deCerteau defines "tactic" as a flexible, nimble action taken by the weak within a space defined and controlled by the strong:

> The place of a tactic belongs to the other. A tactic insinuates itself into the other's place, fragmentarily, without taking it over in its entirety, without being able to keep it at a distance. It has at its disposal no base. . . . Because it does not have a place, a tactic depends on time—it is always on the watch for opportunities that must be seized "on the wing." Whatever it wins, it does not keep. It must constantly manipulate events to turn them into "opportunities." (deCerteau 1984, xix)

Interest-based organizers (like Saul Alinksy and the IAF) argue that tactical actions should be the primary focus of organizing work because they provide the most immediate benefit for the greatest number of people, regardless of the motivations or motives of those involved. Paula Mathieu, in her book *Tactics of Hope*, argues that it is important that educators draw on tactical, rather than strategic, work when engaging in partnerships with communities because only in this way can they ensure that the university's strategic position will not subsume the organization's goals and desires.

In deCerteau's schema, strategy is the opposite of tactics. It is

> the calculus of force-relationships which becomes possible when a subject of will and power (a proprietor, an enterprise, a city, a scientific institution) can be isolated from an "environment." A strategy assumes a place that can be circumscribed as proper . . . and thus serve as the basis for generating relations with an exterior distinct from it (competitors, adversaries, "clienteles," "targets," or "objects" of research). Political, economic, and scientific rationality has been constructed on this strategic model. (1984, xix)

But community organizers see tactics and strategies as more closely aligned than deCerteau's definitions suggest. Erik Peterson, an organizer and trainer for Wellstone Action, says that strategies and tactics are

> cojoined—or at least they should be. A strategy is a road map to build the power necessary to accomplish a purpose . . . and tactics are the tools/actions taken as part of a strategy. Without strategy— without answering the question, "How does this move us toward our goal?", tactics are simply random and unconnected acts. They may disrupt, get attention—but they do not "win." (Peterson 2007)

In other words, for Peterson, strategy is the long-term plan while tactics are the ways that strategy is achieved.

Others, though, draw a sharper distinction between tactics and strategy. NCTE Director Kent Williamson, for example, notes that sometimes educators have made tactical choices that aren't necessarily strategic. As an example, Williamson describes the strategic trade-offs that he believes educators have made in the context of NCLB and the Bush administration's education policies:

> To employ a too-simple dichotomy, I think that our challenges are more strategic than tactical. The orthodoxy among policymakers . . . is that literacy education and teacher education is badly broken—regardless of what data is presented to them. Unfortunately, many education groups are the culprits in spreading this perception, because the standard approach to "winning" more federal/state resources seems to follow a familiar recipe: 1) there is an urgent problem of unprecedented magnitude; 2) fortunately, with a fresh infusion of federal funds, we can fix it; 3) we can accept limits on how the funds will be spent, even if they eliminate or curtail teaching/curricular/assessment approaches that we know to be effective. The consolidation of message about "the problem" is what led to a skewed interpretation of the National Reading Panel report (that in turn brought us Reading First and No Child Left Behind) and is now being re-enacted with an adolescent literacy focus (Striving Readers) and, possibly, higher education (Spellings Commission report). (Williamson 2006)

Williamson's point here is important, and one that WPAs and writing instructors need to consider in story-changing work. Framing our goals within existing strategies, as Williamson suggests, can result in tactical gains—more money for existing programs, new programs themselves. But the strategic costs of tactical gains can be extraordinarily high—high enough, in fact, that they (and we, because we participate in them) undermine the very strategic goals for which we are working in the first place.

Interest-based organizing is the most tactical model here; values-based is the most strategic. Issue-based organizing lies at the midpoint between tactical and strategic work. What is important for WPAs and writing instructors who want to create change is to think about what they gain and lose, tactically and strategically, in making particular choices, and to keep that analysis in mind as they work to change stories.

CHANGING STORIES AND BACKWARD PLANNING

At first glance, it seems like identifying a story *to* change should be the first step that a WPA or writing instructor takes to change stories about writers and writing. Justine, for example, might say she wants to change the perception of writing instruction in her university. But if we stop for a minute and think about the teaching practices of thoughtful instructors whom we know and thoughtful research we have read, we'll probably recognize that there's considerable groundwork to be laid before we address what we want to affect. We don't start planning a class by creating a laundry list of what we want students to do, after all: "I want students to read a source from Sociology Abstracts, and do some ethnographic research, and create a multigenre piece, and summarize and work with surface conventions."

Instead, we plan backward, working from what really are the *strategic*, or long-term, goals of our courses and programs, to short-term ones that could be seen (through the Peterson definition above) as *tactical*. We might say, "I want students to develop their acumen with rhetorical analysis; sharpen their critical thinking, reading, and writing strategies; and enhance their abilities to work with surface conventions. To accomplish this, I'll design assignments that ask them to do X, Y, and Z." Grant Wiggins and Jay McTighe, authors of *Learning by Design*, have described this as "backward design." They propose that teachers identify the desired results, then determine "acceptable evidence" of achievement or learning, and *then* plan learning that will help students achieve those goals (Wiggins and McTighe 1998, 9). In organizing terms, this is strategic thinking and planning—considering the end or the goal, then designing tactics that keep that goal in mind.

Interest-, value-, and issue-based approaches to organizing also contain strategies to take the all-important valuable first step in the story-changing process, and then to move beyond that first step. Each starts from principles held by the WPA and the institution, principles that reflect the passions and interests of those individuals and entities embracing and espousing them. Interest- and issue-based approaches also offer strategies for accessing these interests; a values-based approach offers strategies for working with them. The difference between these approaches is that they outline different endpoints for organizing/story-changing work, and thus reflect approaches to engaging tactics (and, in some cases, strategies).

Interest-Based Organizing

Interest-based organizing is commonly associated with grassroots work. In organizing circles, it is considered the oldest and best-known model of community organizing. Because values- and issue-based approaches extend from and draw on this element of interest-based work, it's important to discuss a bit of its origins, which are firmly rooted in the progressive pragmatism outlined in chapter 2.

Interest-based organizing proceeds from the work of Saul Alinsky, perhaps America's foremost community organizer (Sen 2003). Although others engaged in organizing work before,

Alinsky was the first organizer to codify a "method" for interest-based organizing. Philosopher Lawrence Engel suggests that Alinsky came to this method through his undergraduate and graduate work at the University of Chicago. There he worked with Robert Park and Ernest W. Burgess, both of whom were aligned with the Chicago school of pragmatic sociology. This "school" emanated from and embraced the values and ideals of the progressive pragmatic jeremiad discussed in chapter 2, a jeremiad that was itself rooted in the Chicago-based work of Dewey, Jane Addams, and other Chicago-based progressive reformers. Among the principles that Alinsky took from this work was that sociologists were not to determine action or engage in research per se, but should instead "organize the community for self-investigation" (quoted in Engel 2002, 54).

Alinsky came to prominence as an organizer working in the neighborhood known as Back of the Yards on Chicago's south side, where he eventually founded the Industrial Areas Foundation (IAF). The approach guiding his work and the organizations is encompassed in Alinksy's "Golden Rule": Never do for others what they can do for themselves (Alinsky 1947 passim 190–204). The principles guiding Alinsky's application of this rule reflect the progressive pragmatic jeremiad's fundamental tenets: optimistic faith in the power of individuals' creative intelligence, collectively applied, to obstacles that interfere with the nation's progress toward a virtuous democracy. "Only through organization," Alinsky insisted, "can a people's program be developed," but it must be developed *by the people affected or desiring change*, not by an organizer (Alinsky 1946, 54). The organizer, instead, serves as a conduit to facilitate the development of individuals' creative intelligences individually and in contact with one another, and then to help those individuals articulate a process for change-making that makes sense to them. While affecting change was a primary goal, cultivating individuals' senses of themselves as intelligent actors in a democracy was the goal behind the goal. As Alinsky explained, *the real democratic program is a democratically minded people*—a healthy, active, participating, interested, self-confident people who, through their participation and interest, become informed, educated, and above all develop faith in themselves, their fellow men, and the future. The people themselves are the future. The people themselves will solve each problem that will arise out of a changing world. They will if they, the people, have the opportunity and power to make and enforce the decision instead of seeing that power vested in just a few. No clique, or caste, power group or benevolent administration can have the people's interest at heart as much as the people themselves. (Alinsky 1946, 55, emphasis in original)

Every page in Alinsky's two most influential books, *Reveille for Radicals* and *Rules for Radicals*, attest to his faith in the principles of progressive pragmatism: a powerful belief in the potential of humankind; an unwavering commitment to the potential for organizers ("radicals") to cultivate individuals' creative intelligence so that they would work together to achieve creative democracy; and profound belief that the democracy could and would support the interests of those individuals. In the preface to a reissued edition of *Reveille for Radicals*, for example, he explained that:

In the end [the free-society organizer] has one all-consuming conviction, one belief, one article of faith—a belief in people, a complete commitment to the belief that if people have the power, the opportunity to act, in the long run they will, most of the time, reach the right decision. . . . Believing in people, the radical has the job of organizing people so that they will have the power and opportunity to best meet each unforeseeable future crisis as they move ahead to realize those values of equality, justice, freedom, the preciousness of human life, and all those rights and values propounded by Judeo-Christianity and democratic tradition. Democracy is not an end but the best means toward achieving these values. (Alinsky 1946, xiv–xvi)

"The democratic way of life," Alinsky insisted, "is the most efficient instrument that man can use to cut through the barriers between him and his hopes for the future" (Alinsky 1946, 39).

Today, Alinsky's approach forms the foundation for the work

of the IAF, which is still based in Chicago. IAF organizers work across the country through locally based community organizations, such as the Bay Area Organizing Coalition (BAOC), which serves as IAF organizer Eleanor Milroy's home base. The IAF's interest-based approach to organizing begins with conversation, which allows the organizer to learn about what motivates people and fuels their actions. What makes people angry? Inspires them? Fuels their passions? The interest-based organizer's first goal is to learn, person-by-person, what makes people tick. Then the interest-based organizer begins connecting people to one another through and around their shared mutual interests. The short-term goal of interest-based organizing is action, because action both addresses issues and helps people understand that they have the power to make change (which, in turn, attracts others with the same goals). The long-term goal is to cultivate individuals' senses of power and authority to make change within the culture. As IAF/BAOC organizer Milroy explains,

> The absolute foundation of [the individual and small group meeting] is to get at people's stories, to get at their anger, to get at their self-interest. If we don't do that, then we're just trying to sell the IAF or our organization or sell an issue, or whatever. And that happens sometimes, and we have to catch ourselves all the time. So our work is to really work hard at getting people to share their story. And obviously we have a million aspects to our stories. So that can go from spiritual journey to educational story to economic story, to cultural stories, whatever. (Milroy 2006)

From these stories, as above, interest-based organizers like Milroy learn about individuals' passions, their anger, the things that motivate them through their daily lives.

The goal of hearing stories for organizers like Milroy is to get to peoples' self interest and use this as the basis for forming relationships. IAF Executive Director Edward Chambers explains: "Power takes place in relationships. . . . Seeing clearly that every act of power requires a relationship is the first step toward realizing that the capacity to be affected by another is the other side of the coin named power" (Chambers and Cowan 28). Describing her job as an organizer, Milroy also emphasizes the importance of relationships:

> My job is to take that collective self-interest and be smart enough to figure out how her self-interest connects to his self-interest connects to her self-interest until you have a broader circle that can give you some measure of power, whether it's something very local and very small, to something like changing health care policy in San Francisco. (Milroy 2006)

Through the process of one-on-one or small group discussions called relational meetings, IAF organizers keep their ears and eyes open for two things: *issues,* which lead to definable, winnable fights; and *leaders,* community members who can rally a group to act on the issues. A base for action is formed when individuals form groups around their shared self interests about a specific issue, and leaders help shape the direction that action takes.

The distinction between *issues* and *problems* is crucial for the IAF's work and for WPAs and writing instructors as well. IAF's Chambers describes the difference between issues and problems in his definition of "actions":

> Actions are aimed toward something you can do something about. It's called an issue. Some things are so large as to overwhelm action efforts. These we term "problems," something you can do nothing about. The number of children living in poverty in America is a problem; training for single mothers with children is a possible issue for an organization with some power. The sale and consumption of illegal drugs is a problem; tearing down six specifically identified crack houses in a neighborhood is an issue. The dysfunction of urban public schools is a problem; getting rid of an abusive sixth grade teacher is an issue. Effective actions target issues, not problems. (Chambers and Cowan 84, emphasis added)

Issues, in this conception, emerge from relationships. The organizer doesn't bring them, but hears them. Equally important, issues are definable, specific things that can be changed. This is distinct from problems, the kinds of big picture issues—"perception of writers and writing"; "discussions of plagiarism in the broader culture"; "relationships between written work and dominant cultural values"—that are certainly there, but are headbangingly frustrating. Identifying issues (not problems) for story-changing work is crucial. With an issue, it's possible to identify a goal, a definition of what success will look like. Success—accomplishing what it is we wanted to do—is crucial for encouraging participation. And while our professional ethos may to some extent value Sisyphus-like efforts to fight the good fight, efforts that seem never to achieve what they've set out to do can sap the energies of even the most enthusiastic person.

With issues, a goal is clear. Issues also lend themselves to specific, focused strategies, which in turn can lead to the sharing of responsibilities for implementation among a variety of people. This again helps to increase participation and buy-in, and distribute the workload of the change-making effort among a broader group. And issues extend from conversations and relationships, *not* from the interests of the organizer (in our case, the WPA or writing instructor). Chambers explains, "issues follow relationships. You don't pick targets and mobilize first; you connect people in and around their interests" (46).

Once issues have emerged from relationships and conversation, the interest-based organizer next identifies leaders who can shape approaches to and action on the issue. Leaders aren't necessarily "names" in the community. Instead, as Milroy explains, a "good leader is . . . someone who has a lot of relationships that people respect and listen to, not necessarily who is the best educated [or] most articulate—they're the people who seem to know a lot of other people and understand their motivations." Identifying leaders is another of the IAF's primary goals. As Eleanor Milroy explains, one measure of success comes

> when this work truly becomes transformative—people who don't see themselves as public people, who haven't been invested in,

people who . . . people say, "Why do you want to talk to me? I'm just a mom." I hear that all the time. All the time. "I'm just a mom." Well, what have we done, for crying out loud, to support that kind of thinking that they're "just a mom?" (Milroy 2006)

"Just moms," "just" people in the community . . . these are the leaders that the IAF seeks to develop.

But IAF organizers aren't as concerned about *why* people are interested in making change—what's important for them is the short-term, tactical actions rather than the long-term, strategic goals. As a result, their focus on *issues* and *relationships* sometimes produces surprising foci and alliances. Milroy says that she initially wrestled with the idea, but has come to recognize the value of this approach through her experience with the IAF.

There's an article that we use called "The Importance of Being Unprincipled." And when I first saw the title I said, "What do you mean? Of course I'm principled." But . . . we want people to do the right thing, even if it's for the wrong reasons. And so we aren't going to get into motive, as long as the end result is what leaders are fighting for. So for example, we've had some key business people who we have fought against like sons-of-guns. But in one case, [one of these people] was getting toward the end of his career, and it was legacy time. How did he want to be remembered? And he was a major banker—major. Well, it turned out that he became our major champion of this job training initiative we were doing [in El Paso]—and I think it was because of his legacy. And I think . . . so people, we're at different points in our lives and we get impacted by different things. In some ways, that's the hardest part of this work is to not stereotype and not make assumptions and to withhold judgment, even though we may have a history with someone that we know is not so good. But we've got to give people room for change, we've got to give ourselves room for change, or we get into this narrow, rigid, . . . we just keep on going the way we were going. (Milroy 2006)

In this story Milroy brings to life Alinsky's commitment to nimbleness of the organizer, whom Alinsky stressed must be "loose, resilient, fluid, and on the move in a society which is itself in a state of constant change. To the extent that he is free from the shackles of dogma, he can respond to the realities of the widely different situations our society presents" (Alinsky 1946, 11).

Engaging in relational conversations, identifying issues through those conversations, and identifying leaders (who can then bring others into action on the issue) are the three fundamental steps of the base- and relationship-building process used by interest-based organizers like those in the IAF. The next steps are to develop a message about the issue to take action on it and to assess the result, processes that are discussed in the next chapter. Ultimately, though, *all* interest-based organizing activities must lead to action, because action both leads to change and draws attention to the organizing effort.

Summary: Interest-Based Organizing

Key elements involved with an interest-based approach to organizing are:

Holding relational meetings to identify interests and form relationships. One-on-one and in small groups, holding conversations to learn about what inspires, motivates, and angers people is crucial for learning about what inspires them, motivates them, and where their passions lie. Edward Chambers lists some simple questions for these kinds of meetings: What do you do? Why do you do what you do? What inspires you? What makes you angry? Why? How?

Identifying issues, not problems, to connect people to and through their interests. In interest-based organizing, the role of the organizer is to listen carefully to hear the issues that emerge from conversations with community members and leaders. What is important to them, and why? What are some *specific* issues that might emerge from concerns? One of the central principles of interest-based (and other) organizing is that *action* attracts support;

identifying issues that can lead to action (and, ideally, victory) is important for building and sustaining a movement.

Identifying and developing leaders. Who in the community might take leadership on these issues? What kinds of research, mobilizing, or involvement actions might be developed based on these issues? How can these actions cultivate leaders and lead to greater involvement among the community? As with identifying issues and taking action, both short-term and long-term goals are embedded in the idea of cultivating leadership.

Building alliances. As Alinsky, Chambers, and Milroy all point out, power comes in relationships, in alliance. The more that are involved in addressing an issue—regardless of their motivations *for* that work—the better.

Mobilizing leaders and community members to take action. As Alinsky said, "change means movement. Movement means friction" (Alinsky 1971, 21). Movement and change are necessary to attract attention—and attract supporters. At the same time, IAF regional director Ernesto Cortes cautions against an overemphasis on mobilization because it might imply that the bulk of the responsibility for action rests on individuals, rather than on a shared commitment by individuals and institutions. "An overemphasis on mobilization," he warns, "can increase the pressures" on the institutions that *do* remain to facilitate social action, "rather than counteract them" (Cortes 2006, 51).

Assessing action and identifying next steps. "What worked? What didn't? What needs to be repeated? What should happen differently next time?" These are key questions for the organizer, who is what we might call, drawing on Donald Schon, a "reflective practitioner." It's important to reiterate that interest-based organizing extends from conversations facilitated *by* the organizer, not *from* the organizer's own agenda (beyond a desire to facilitate good work). So while I make the case that it is important to identify principles, we might not draw from or refer explicitly to these principles save for general guideline for ourselves.

Returning to Justine's situation, it's useful to think about how interest-based strategies might be useful for addressing her dilemmas. Perhaps the first thing that the savvy reader might note is that interest-based organizing doesn't offer particularly handy quick-fix strategies for situations like hers. It relies on alliance building, and that takes time. But her situation does present occasions for that building. Justine might talk with the chair and the dean, but in an interest-based conversation she would be not pushing her own agenda. Instead she would learn about their passions and interests—given the context, perhaps about *academic* passions and interests—like writing. The purpose of the conversation would not be to promote a perspective or view, but to listen for moments of anger, intensity, commitment (maybe about writing-related issues, or maybe about something else entirely). Then Justine might engage in similar conversations with other stakeholders and interested parties—other faculty, students, administrators, writing instructors—and listen for similar passions and issues. Her goal would be to connect these individuals around these issues, rather than advancing any perspective of their own. The interest-based organizer always seeks to cultivate individuals' interests and passions and use them as the basis for accessing and cultivating creative intelligence, then to help individuals put that creative intelligence to work by identifying and creating solutions for overcoming obstacles interfering with their own happiness and, by extension, their ability to contribute to the health of the democracy.

As this example makes clear, putting elements of an interest-based approach to organizing into WPA practice might lead us to shift the focus of our work somewhat. It might, for instance, involve talking to a group of people—people inside of the writing program, those outside of it—about their passions, their concerns, and their interests. These *might* be related to writing; they also might be related to a host of issues or concerns that are seemingly unrelated to writing. The WPA, acting as an organizer, might then bring people together around these issues and identify actions that could be taken to address them, then engage in the mobilizing and assessment activities implicit in interest-based organizing work. The advantages of interest-based organizing, then, are that it facilitates the development of communities aligned around individual and collective interests; the identification and development of leaders within the community; the decentralization of power and mobilization, spreading it throughout the community; and increased investment by community members in the long-term development of the community.

As with all of these approaches, an interest-based approach also presents some potential challenges that WPAs and writing instructors should also consider. Many stem from the fact that interest-based organizing models were not intended for systems as explicitly hierarchical and interest-focused as academe. For instance, interest-based organizers mobilize communities and leaders around issues that emerge *from relational meetings*, not from their own agendas. The WPA's agenda, in other words, becomes *mobilizing others around their interests*, not mobilizing others around *her* interests. Additionally, interest-based organizing focuses on tactical action, taking a very long view of the notion of strategy. Interest-based organizing, as Eleanor Milroy says, is about "doing the right thing, even if it's for the wrong reasons." The presumption in this organizing model is that those "right things" will eventually, over a period of time, lead to strategic change—but this is a long, slow process. As we'll see below, other organizing models and activists believe that engaging in this kind of tactics-focused work has resulted in progressives putting themselves in a corner that it's hard to emerge from, so that achieving those long-term goals is especially difficult.

QUESTIONS TO FACILITATE AN INTEREST-BASED APPROACH TO ORGANIZING

Since interest-based work proceeds from conversation, questions to facilitate this approach focus on before- and after-conversation.

Before Conversation

Who are potential allies for your writing program? With whom might you be interested in forming relationships? For each person/entity (e.g., department) that you list, be sure to note why they are of interest to you.

What might be useful questions to learn about these people/entities? What might you ask to learn about what motivates them, what inspires them, what makes them angry?

After Conversation

What did you learn? What inspires/angers/motivates this person or entity?

What issues/problems seem especially important to this person/entity?

Who are others who might share this interest?

How might you put these people into communication with one another around their common interests?

What resources exist (on your campus, in the community, etc.) to facilitate action around this interest?

VALUES-BASED ORGANIZING

Values-based organizing stems from the recent extension of linguistic theory, especially the concept of framing, into organizing work. George Lakoff and the Rockridge Institute have been at the forefront of this approach. Shaping the message,

setting out terms for discussion, determining the direction—
these are all central to values-based organizing. In this sense,
a values-based approach is focused on long-term strategy (as
opposed to the focus on short-term tactics in interest-based
models). A base for action is developed when people come
together in and through their values, their principles, and
use those values as a basis for shifting frames around issues
important to them. Lakoff and Rockridge colleagues explain
that in this values-based model "issues are secondary—not
irrelevant or unimportant, but secondary. A position on issues
should follow from one's values, and the choice of issues and
policies should symbolize those values" (Lakoff 2006, 8). The
idea here is that people come together in and around their
values, not issues, but that through these values-based coalitions issues emerge.

George Lakoff, whose work is prominently featured in this
approach, has long been interested in the ways that human
beings use metaphors to shape their approaches to the world.[2]
In *Metaphors We Live By*, Lakoff laid out an analysis of cognitive
processes, arguing that human beings are hardwired with some
fundamental value systems. These systems lead to metaphors
through which we experience the world, such as the nurturing parent and the strict father metaphors. A later book, *Moral
Politics*, analyzed the ways in which these two metaphors led
humans to interact in political arenas. In what Lakoff has since
identified as the *Moral Politics* model, he explained that the strict
father and the nurturant parent "produce two fundamentally
opposed moral systems for running a nation—two ideologies
that specify not only how the nation should be governed by also,
in many respects, how we should live our lives" (Lakoff 2006,
50). Growing from this work, in 2004 Lakoff became frustrated
with the Democrats' seeming inability to take smart and strategic action (especially during the election cycle). He authored a
short, accessible book called *Don't Think of an Elephant!: Know
Your Values and Frame the Debate* that distilled analysis and ideas
from the two previous books. The book became wildly popular

and has been used by many candidates, especially on the left, as a framework for action.

Of the three models discussed here, values-based organizing is the newest; as such, there are fewer examples of this model in action from which to draw. However, a number of organizations are incorporating values-based ideas in their work, such as MoveOn.org. As MoveOn founder Joan Blades explains,

> [MoveOn] started with a petition [for Congress to move on after the Clinton impeachment hearings] that went viral. We sent it out to 100 of our friends and families and it grew to a half million people. . . . And the process was very much a dialogue with the MoveOn members. [Members] are letting us know what they care about in all sorts of ways all the time, and our job at MoveOn is to listen— really well—and combine that with what opportunities there are to act on . . . issues. So it's not us telling them what to do, so much as them telling us what they're interested in and then [engaging that interest] in meaningful ways. . . . It is about giving up yourself for your ideals, and that's what MoveOn members are doing. (Blades 2005, emphasis added)

In other words, according to Blades, MoveOn members come for the values and define issues from there. Michel Gelobter, executive director of Redefining Progress, also describes the importance of focusing on values:

> If we win, as we just did, a huge victory on climate in California and in that victory is embedded the potential of a charge—a polluter pay system for California where the polluter would have to pay for their emissions—that is a big piece of what we worked on in that legislation, and that's great. But if five years from now, if we have to implement it and we still can't say "gas tax" without being laughed out of the room, we're not winning the values battle. (Gelobter 2006)

Blades's and Gelobter's statements illustrate a premise embedded in the values-based approach to organizing: unless action proceeds from values, the long-term strategic objectives won't be met. Anat Shenker-Osorio, a former Rockridge researcher and a cofounder of Real Reason (a language policy institute in San Francisco), explains that these ideas are activated through language, and that's why working in language is especially important. Shenker-Osorio describes how language establishes the terms of a frame:

> How you have a society in which there is opportunity for all, like how that works, at any level, how it makes sense that it's not a zero sum game, how what the nature of the reciprocal relationship is between government and citizens, what taxes are, what having your latte and still being environmentally friendly—what that even means or looks like, how that works in society, is not even worked out. It's not worked out at the level of "How does that even work?"
>
> On the right . . . there's a model . . . that makes sense, and it goes straight back to . . . a [cognitive] predisposition toward individualism. . . . We really feel like the basic thought structures of how the world is supposed to work, when you are working from a set of predispositions on the left, is not very clear. . . . I want to live in a society with opportunity for all. But I can't even describe to you . . . at a mathematical model level, even—and I'm not even talking policy—how that would work. . . .
>
> The competitive model is so well understood and so well activated. We can say words like "cooperation" or "inclusion," but I don't think people understand—and I include myself—what that actually means. How would that work? Would the stores have less things? Are prices cheaper? What happens? (Shenker-Osorio 2006)

Through language, values-based organizers believe, people can discover and articulate the values at the core of their central beliefs. This approach lies behind commonly used communication strategies, for instance when groups are asked to "imagine the headline at the end of your campaign" (see chapter 5 for more on this and other activities). The assumption is that, by playing with potential language, groups can explore their beliefs. At the same time, also embedded in this model is the premise that the wrong word or choice of words can activate the wrong frame. This is the theory behind Lakoff's reminder that "a word is defined relatively to [a] frame. When we negate a frame, we evoke a frame" (Lakoff 2004, 3). In other words, say what you want, not what you don't want. What the left has failed to do, these analysts argue, is address the values at the core of people's beliefs.

Once individuals and organizations have come together around language that activates and reflects their values, the next step in values-based organizing is to present those values in public settings. Lakoff argues that a number of frames must be used in combination for the purpose. First are deep frames, "moral values and principles that cut across issues and that are required before any slogans or clever phrases can resonate with the public," such as the idea that all citizens should have the opportunity to participate in democracy on their own terms (Lakoff 2006, xii). Next are argument frames, frames that reflect the values of deep frames and can be used to frame discussions of multiple issues, like the case that all students should have equal access to higher education (Lakoff 2006, 124–25). Then come surface frames, also referred to in a derogatory way as "spin," the surface frame that is put on top of issues (Lakoff 2006, 124–25). Last are messaging frames, the semantic frames established within genres that outline roles (such as "messengers, audience, issue, message, medium, and images") (Lakoff 2006, 36).

The Opportunity Agenda (OA), a public policy advocacy institute, provides numerous publications and announcements (through its listserv and Web site) that illustrate values-based frames in action. For example, in a "communications toolkit" collaboratively developed with the Strategic Press Information Network (SPIN) Project, OA lays out the "dimensions of opportunity" that they propose serve as the deep frames of the progressive position, and then show how those frames can be extended to argument, surface, and messaging frames. For instance, one element of their deep frame is "mobility," the ability to advance beyond one's current station and participate in economic and civic life (2006, 6). The deep frame of "mobility" can be translated into argument frames in multiple discussions—higher education, economic access, wages, housing, and so on. Surface frames can also invoke the concept of mobility, such as the statement, "Because the SAT writing exam is a high-stakes test privileging one genre, and that genre reflects particular values, it denies students the promise of mobility extended through higher education." Surface frames like this one also imply messaging frames—particular roles and players in the message.

Summary: Values-Based Organizing

Where an interest-based approach has organizers facilitating conversations to identify others' interests and passions, values-based approaches proceed from the assumption that individuals will unite around values that reflect their interests. The values of the organizer, as the convener of discussions, play a more prominent role here, since she must work from those values (which themselves reflect her principles). Further, a values-based approach proceeds from the idea that language—in the form of metaphors and frames—can be used to trigger particular conceptions of individuals' principles and values. Among the three models discussed here, values-based organizing is the most long-term and strategic of the models. Interest-based work begins with concrete issues that are immediate to peoples' experiences; values-based organizing starts with the conceptual notion of values, and then works backward to issues. Values are the core of the organizing effort, and tactics are always designed with the strategy in mind. In terms of the tactics-strategies trajectory, then, values-based organizing has the most immediate potential for affecting strategy and frame; however, the trade-off is that operating within this model may mean compromises with regard to tactics that could result in short-term loss (or loss of the tactical alliances that such actions can create).

A values-based approach to organizing involves:

Identifying values important for individuals and organizations (such as the WPA or writing program). Values are always central to the organizing effort, and issues extend from them.

Identifying others who share the same values. Values can serve as points where people come together as they discover common values, or individuals holding the values can extend those values to others and invite them to participate in them.

Developing frames that reflect values, and using those frames to shape issues. Framing is key here, and working through the values reflected in frames ensures that the values reflected in the frame remain prominent.

As with all of these models, values-based organizing holds advantages and disadvantages for WPAs. It is the most strategic, big picture, and long-term of the approaches described here. Its focus on articulating deeply held values and building alliances around those means that WPAs and writing instructors have the potential to articulate their visions and their values, ideally in concert with others who share those same values. Returning to the dilemmas posed in Justine's scenario, values-based organizing presents different strategies for change-making work. First, Justine would identify her own values and use these as a starting point. Then she would consider the frame surrounding writing instruction, perhaps by learning the viewpoints of individuals on her campus that she wanted to affect. Then she would consider the connections between frequently used terms (like "remediation" or "process") and the larger metaphors to which they are connected by examining other uses of these terms in education-related contexts, perhaps by invoking the conceptions of code words and excess meanings described in chapter 1. Justine could then use this analysis to propel her frame-changing actions. She might analyze alternative conceptions of writers and writing that they want to advance, and consider terms (words, metaphors, frames) to advance these conceptions. Again, she could then turn to the research and the language corpora, examining the uses of these terms in other contexts. The goal of this work would be to consider what values might be triggered by these "deep frames" in order to consider their usefulness for her purposes, changing the conception of writers and writing held by those administrators. Once she developed a set of frames that they considered successful and useful, Justine could craft different kinds of messages (written, verbal, and otherwise) reflecting these frames to advance a consistent message that reflected their shared values. In the short term, these frames might or might not affect the immediate dilemmas they face; the presumption is that they would have considerable effect in the long term.

Perhaps because it grows out of academic work, values-based organizing is also the most conventionally academic of these models. It's possible to dig into and spend a lot of time thinking through the theoretical premises of the work (such as whether values are really hardwired—cognitive linguists like Lakoff say yes; more culturally oriented theorists, like Stuart Hall or Norman Fairclough, would say no), which some of us could spend years discussing. But this, of course, appeals and speaks primarily to academics. For this reason, it is a disadvantage of this approach (e.g., it might contribute to the narrative, discussed in chapters 1 and 3, that academics do not understand the nature of the virtuous democracy and, therefore, their actions have little relevance for preparing students to participate in it).

Values-based organizing also holds some other challenges. As the most strategic of the three models, a hard-line values-based approach might mean enormous tactical losses. Scholars of educational structures (e.g., Miller 1998 Palmer 1998; O'Reilley 2005a; Thompson 2005) have made compelling arguments about surviving the bureaucratic, hierarchical realities of the educational system (K-16). As Miller argues, success in this system is based on imperfect compromise, and to think otherwise is to live in an unreal world (Miller 1998). As the newest of the three models discussed here, values-based organizing is also simultaneously the best and least well-conceptualized. The theoretical basis of the work is clearly well developed in the academic literature, but the extension of that work to action is less realized.

However, the potential weak points in this approach should not lead WPAs and writing instructors who want to change stories to cast aside this model entirely: there are important elements here to which we must attend. Chief among these is the need to develop, and work from, a vision of what we *want*, not what we *do not* want. As the OA's Executive Director Alan Jenkins said in a presentation I attended, "Martin Luther King never said, 'I have a critique'" (Jenkins 2006). As academics, we are well trained to argue *against*. We are far less expert at arguing *for*, at expressing a vision of what we *want* and why we think it is important. And Shenker-Osorio, Rockridge scholars, and linguists like Geoffrey Nunberg argue that a vision *of the possible* (not of the not-feasible, difficult, or unrealistic) must be developed in and through carefully chosen language—whether you buy the argument that this language activates either cognitive processes or cultural patterns. The key to change, argues Nunberg, is asserting *stories*—narratives—about the purpose of education and how our work is important in it. Strategically it also is wise to consider how these narratives are linked to others, like those stemming from the progressive pragmatic jeremiad. Values-based organizing provides strategies for asking questions about these concepts and their historical and ideological antecedents. If the words (narratives, stories, metaphors) that we use do tap into elements of that jeremiad, what are we invoking? Do the (deep, argument, surface, and other) frames in our language reflect the values that we want to advance? Developing stories and working from them also serves as a grounding point in values, in the kinds of principles that can underscore our work for change.

QUESTIONS TO FACILITATE VALUES-BASED ORGANIZING

Based on your own analysis, what are the principles or values that are central to your work as a writing instructor or WPA?

What issues do you see as central to your writing program (e.g., class size, instructor qualifications, instructor salaries, control over curriculum, etc.)? List the three most important ones.

    a.

    b.

    c.

To whom are these issues important (e.g., you, instructors in the program, administrators, etc.)?

What values do you see extending from the relevant issues that you have identified? For this, you might refer to the principles that underscore your approach to WPA and teaching work. For example, if one of the issues that you identified is "class size," you might extend that to a value of "individual opportunity." Remember that values need to cross *multiple* issues.

Who else might also participate in the *values* that you have identified as linked to your issues, and why might they participate in them (e.g., what is their motivation)?

What are the key words and phrases in those values? How else have they been used, by whom, and for what purposes? Might you need to restate/reframe your values based on this analysis?

What questions might you ask of potential allies, or what overtures might you make to them, to involve them in organizing efforts around one of the issues you (or they) have identified as extending from values?

ISSUE-BASED ORGANIZING

Traditional issue-based organizing is likely familiar. Someone—a political candidate, the leader of a union or a political party—identifies and defines issues upon which to take action (with varying degrees of input) and forms an agenda or a platform based on those issues. Through existing (and sometimes hierarchical) structures, people under that leadership take action. However, they do not have a prominent voice in shaping those issues.

Wellstone Action (WA), a Minnesota-based organization formed after the death of Senator Paul Wellstone, both uses and continually develops a new version of issue-based organizing for its work training grassroots activists and political candidates. These trainings typically take place in a "Camp Wellstone," an intensive, three-day institute. Camp Wellstones are held around the country throughout the year. WA also offers advanced camps for those who have already been through the initial training, as well as "training the trainer" sessions for organizers. WA has a long list of "successes"—candidates who have participated in Camp Wellstone and been elected to political office, college students across the country who have participated in Campus Camp Wellstones, and grassroots activists who have attended the "organizing" strand of Camp Wellstone. (WA also offers Camp Sheila Wellstone sessions, which focus specifically on advocating for the rights of women and children.)

For WA, organizing work is a three-part activity that consists of developing a base in and through individuals' interests, considering the long-term policy consequences and implications of the base, and working on affecting the electoral system to accommodate and affect the short- and long-term goals extending from interests and long-term implications. In this sense, issue-based organizing blends elements of interest- and values-based approaches. There *are* issues here, as WA organizer Erik Peterson explains, "I always start with the question: what are we facing and where do we want to move? This is what we are focused on—we come out of an issue or an agenda-based position. There is an agenda." So while "there is an agenda" in issue-based organizing, issue-based groups like WA seek to extend beyond that issue to values and interests (Peterson 2007).

To explain the relationship between issues, policy, and political work, WA uses a triangle where pieces are connected, and sometimes in tension with one another:

FIGURE 1

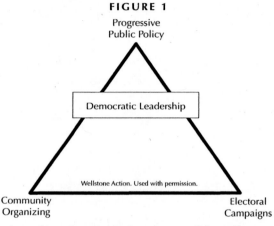

Progressive
Public Policy

Democratic Leadership

Wellstone Action. Used with permission.

Community
Organizing

Electoral
Campaigns

In an issue-based approach to organizing, issues serve as the magnet that attracts people to the cause, as is the case with interest-based work. But issue-based organizers like those associated with WA don't see making progress on or "solving" those issues as the *endpoint* of issue-based organizing, as interest-based approaches sometimes do. Instead these issues serve as the beginning point of a long-term process that involves extending from interests to values, as in a values-based approach. In this way, issue-based approaches also involve moving from short-term goals (tactics) within the context of longer-term ones (strategies). To that end, WA organizer Erik Peterson explains, issue agendas are starting points. From them, issue-based organizers seek to develop relationships, like interest-based organizers, but unlike interest-based work these relationships are designed to achieve short-term (tactical) success *and* targeted, long-term (strategic) change.

Relationship building is the long-term part of organizing which co-exists with and helps build for issue-organizing. This relationship building is at the heart of what we [WA] talk about when we talk about community organizing and base-building. . . . Too often [community organizing, base building, and electoral campaigns] are seen as oppositional or unconnected activities. (Peterson 2006)

As the WA organizing triangle implies, relationship building can begin at one of several points. As in an interest-based approach, it might start with an individual's (self-)interest, as Peterson suggests above, especially as that person's interest is represented through stories. In this sense, issue-based organizing draws on strategies used by interest-based organizers, like conducting meetings to hear about peoples' passions and interests. Alternatively it can also stem from values, and the organizer might listen for or identify values that seem central to the individual or organization. Wherever the starting point, base-building is also central for issue-based organizing. Here, though, the key is to balance short-term interests and long-term goals. As Peterson explains, action—"what are we facing and where do we want to move"—is a starting place.

Like interest-based organizers, WA also encourages groups or organizations to conduct a power analysis as they identify issues and mobilize for action. In a power analysis organizations analyze who the "core constituencies" are on whom they can count for support; who are likely allies they might target for mobilization; who are likely opponents of the group, organization, or action (and why); and who might be the primary and secondary targets—that is, the "individuals or groups that *actually* make a decision about your issue/program," and "the individuals or groups that influence the primary targets" (Peterson 2007). The challenge comes if organizations try to mobilize people around issues *without* base-building. As Erik Peterson explains:

In the labor movement we often focus on mobilizing people: for example, we need 15 people for a picket line, we need 50 people for a rally; we need X people for this action or that one. We need

you to contribute X dollars to Y. And when they don't volunteer or
don't contribute, we oftentimes blame members for not caring or
being apathetic, or blame the staff for not working hard enough
or for not caring or being on program. But it's really because the
union hasn't done its work: we need to organize before we focus on
how to mobilize. (Peterson 2007)

Analyzing the strengths, weaknesses, opportunities, and
threats for the organization and situating these within an analysis of larger power structures is also an important part of issue-
based organizing. The key difference between that strategy and
issue-based work, especially as it is enacted by WA, is the extension from issues and (self-)interests to values. This difference
emerges in the distinction that Peterson makes between *organizing conversations* (which are intended to build relationships, add
to the base, and move people to and around long-term values
that are important for them) and *mobilizing conversations* (which
are intended to motivate members of the base to advocate for
particular issues or causes that they have *already identified* as
important to them).

FIGURE 2

Organizing Conversations	Mobilizing Conversations
Intentional conversations that go deeply into a person's: Issues—what we act on Values—principles, things we care deeply about Interests—things we have a stake in	Prompted conversations that aim to connect an issue with a person's interests, anger, and hope Find points of common concern; make a link between the person's problem and the solution (the campaign) that leads them to take some action (vote, volunteer, contribute, etc.)

Wellstone Action. Used by permission.

Again, there are connections between this portion of issue-
based organizing and the interest-based strategies of groups like
the IAF. It is predicated on the formation of relationships; like
all of the models discussed here, it also puts self-interest at the
center of mobilizing or base-building work. But it also quickly
puts that self-interest to work in the service of a larger issue that
represents and reflects a larger, strategic position identified by

a candidate, an organization, or a leadership, and that issue serves as the point for mobilization. In a follow-up interview after reading a draft of this chapter, Peterson reflected on the ways that WA blends existing strategies and pulls from interest- and values-based work:

> There's an IAF [interest-based] component to our training, and we [also] talk about values and reframing the debate. Issues come and go—that's the transitory nature of [them]—and we talk about that. You can't build long-term progressive power around an issues-based agenda. It has to be connected to interests and communities, and grounded in a moral vision of the world. It has to be values-based. The power of the agenda comes from values and that connection. When we talk about messaging, we always talk about it as a conversation with folks that is grounded in values. You lead with those values, and that story, as opposed to leading with the issue. Why do people vote against their best interests? Who says they did? They voted against issues, perhaps, that went contrary to their material well-being—but who says that's the most important thing in their self-interest? . . . We locate ourselves . . . somewhere in this continuum—where we can freely grab. But ultimately, we go back to tactics and strategy. With tactics and strategy, we see strategy . . . really as longer term and in some ways it's the road map of how you achieve your goal. It's the broader plan, [and] the tactics are the tools that you use to get there. Strategy deals with much more the larger picture, and tactics are included within the strategy. The tactics feed into an overall strategy. A tactic might be that we're going to march on the boss—hold a rally. [But we ask the] strategic question: how does that move us to power, change the power and relationships, to achieve that end? [We] draw on the realm of tactics—mobilize, create energy. But the question is, [only employing tactics,] do you actually move or hold power that moves an agenda? (Peterson 2007)

Summary: Issue-Based Organizing

The approach to issue-based organizing reflected in WA's work blends elements of interest- and values-based approaches.

Issue-based organizing involves:

Working from an agenda that addresses issues of concern for the group. Issue-based work has an agenda; however, that agenda is flexible and accommodates (as much as possible) the interests of constituents and allies within long-term, strategic goals.

Listening to and working with the ideas and interests of a base of supporters. Who is among the core constituencies, and what are their interests? What about potential allies? What do they see as strengths, challenges, opportunities, and threats? What are their interests in these issues?

Using short-term goals (tactics) to achieve long-term objectives (strategies), and situating these within values. Issue-based organizing asks how individuals can be brought into work for long-term, values-based change through short-term campaigns. How can a base sharing common values and interests be expanded and mobilized?

Working strategically, through a series of steps, to conduct analyses and plan action. Strength, weakness, opportunity, and threat (SWOT) and power analyses are important steps to action for the issue-based organizer, as is the process of shaping and communicating messages described in the next chapter.

Some elements of issue-based organizing probably also feel familiar to WPAs and writing instructors. Justine's dilemma illustrates that there are a lot of issues stemming from dilemmas WPAs and writing instructors typically face, and there are many issues underscoring those dilemmas that could be tackled by the activist WPA. Often we see our roles as defining and advancing positions *on* issues, as well. After all, as the discussion in chapter 1 about principles and actions illustrate, we're motivated by some pretty strong emotions and firm principles that lead us to want to take action. But the issue-based approach described here also can provide a framework that we can use to temper our own commitment and think systematically about how to work *from* it, not necessarily *through* it, to connect with others. Again, that work starts with conversation, as in interest-based organizing; it also involves learning about and connecting to peoples' values, as in values-based work. Embedded in these conversations, of course, are our own principles, beliefs, and values—and hopefully we can connect to others around those.

QUESTIONS TO FACILITATE ISSUE-BASED ORGANIZING

What are the principles or values that are central to your writing program?

What issues (not problems!) do you see as central to your writing program? (e.g., class size, instructor qualifications, instructor salaries, control over curriculum, etc.) List the three most important ones.

    a.

    b.

    c.

What are the connections between these (short term) issues and the values that you have identified as important?

To whom are these issues important? (e.g., you, instructors in the program, administrators, etc.)

What individuals and groups do you see as important for supporting your writing program mission? What are their motivations and their interests in your issues?

What questions might you ask of individuals and groups to initiate a discussion around your common interests?

What short-term (tactical) actions might you take, ideally with allies identified above, and how will they be integrally connected to long-term (strategic) goals and values?

SUMMARY: ORGANIZING MODELS

While there are differences between interest-, values-, and issue-based approaches to organizing, they are all rooted in the progressive pragmatic jeremiad (and, in many ways, in the work of Saul Alinsky [e.g., Sen 2003, xliv]). All invest enormous faith in the power of individuals to cultivate creative intelligence; all try to facilitate dialogue and action with the intent of making change; all believe that these processes of dialogue-facilitating and change-making, and the changes that result from the processes, will ultimately move the nation closer to the achievement of a just democracy. All also (implicitly or explicitly) address some of the shortcomings of progressive pragmatism addressed by West and others, like the lack of immediate attention to material conditions such as class, race, and gender (Sen 2003, xlv–xlvii).

All of these approaches engage in this work through some common steps as well. The first step involves identifying the principles that we hold important. What are our values? What do we believe, and why do we believe what we do? A values-based model would have us work from these principles consistently and without compromise; an interest-based model would have us understand them and put them into dialogue with more pragmatic exigencies of "everyday life," and an issue-based approach would have us land somewhere in the middle between these two positions. Nevertheless, understanding principles (even if the principle is that short-term gain and tactical action is the most important goal) is the starting point for this work.

The next step is thinking about goals and allies. What do we want to do? Who are our allies? How can we reach out to them? Through an interest-based model we would engage in relational conversations to learn about others' interests and attempt to form coalitions among those interests (and, perhaps, our own); a values-based model would suggest that we should plan conversations and activities that might allow us to form coalitions around shared values; and an issue-based approach would suggest that we might investigate potential allies' passions and work from them to bring them on board with an agenda that both reflects and might be further shaped by our shared values.

A third consideration is how we want to approach the work *of* that change? How can elements of these three models (and additional ones) facilitate efforts to establish and further develop a base? While each of these models provides different motivations for and approaches to this development, all put a premium on dialogue, conversation, and listening. This is because each acknowledges that we can't go it alone—building alliances, whether with those who share our short-term interests or our long-term visions, is absolutely crucial to achieving change. Connecting people in and through self-interests is a crucial part of building a base, another feature common to all of these models. The base is a core, but it also must be constantly evolving and expanding to form the nexus of change-making efforts. Sociologist William Gamson points to key reasons why people join social movements, all of which speak to the notion of self-interest—they find places where their personal visions and skills are enhanced, but they also connect those visions and skills to larger visions and consciousnesses (Gamson 1991, 38–41). Each of these models recognizes the importance of developing leaders and expanding the base through these connections.

The questions that emerge, then, are about how to develop a vision: Collectively and organically from a group of stakeholders, as in interest-based organizing? Reflecting a set of shared values held by a group, as in values-based work? Or through an agenda that is open to amendment based on the input of others sharing the same vision, as in issue-based organizing? Each present different opportunities and different challenges. No one is better than any other; each is useful for different purposes and different goals.

If the actions and activities embedded in these models feel familiar, it's because so many of them are involved in the work we already do. As in so many cases, in fact, adapting these models for WPA work is less a matter of developing new skills and more one of repurposing those we already have. As I suggested above, for instance, the kinds of questions that interest-based organizers ask in relational meetings are quite similar to those that we might ask on student papers: Could you tell me more? Could you help me understand? The literature on commenting (e.g., Sommers 1982; Straub and Lunsford 1995; Straub 1996; Smith 1997) provides numerous examples of effective (and ineffective) comments, and an examination of why particular questions are more (and less) useful for developing student work; the commenting approaches discussed there are reminiscent of the kinds of questions involved in relational meetings.

Another element of organizing involves listening—to what fires people up, what makes them mad, how they understand the world. This impulse, too, can be located in the scholarly literature. Peter Elbow has written extensively about listening with students as they write (see, for example, "High Stakes and Low Stakes" and "Getting Along"); Glynda Hull and Mike Rose's "This Wooden Shack Place" remains a touching and important testament to the importance of letting people define their own perspectives and ideas rather than imposing judgments on those ideas based on our own perceptions or perspectives. As discussed in chapter 1, pedagogies that build on the germinal work of scholars like Mary Rose O'Reilley, Parker Palmer, and Paolo Freire also expand on the idea of listening to and working with students' ideas as a central part of a dialogic educational process. "There is no knowing (that is, connecting one thing to another) something that is not at the same time a 'communication of the something known," Freire explained in his final book, *Pedagogy of Freedom*. "There is no intelligibility that is not at the same time communication and intercommunication, and that is not grounded in dialogue" (Freire 1998, 42). This dialogue emerges—"produced by learners, in common with the teacher responsible for their education"—and enables the development of meeting points where learners and teachers are transformed (Freire 1998, 46). This is the process of conscientization, an awareness of one's self and the unfinished nature of that self in relation to others and to the world (56).

Building alliances, too, is a practice familiar to many writing instructors. An illustration of this kind of work can be found, for instance, in the assessment-focused WPA work discussed in chapter 1. The reconceived notion of validity proposed by O'Neill and Huot, for example, requires assessments to identify and consider what assessments are being done, for what reasons, and with what effects. Huot also advocates bringing others—stakeholders in the program from a variety of constituencies—into the assessment process. By engaging in this kind of public discussion of writing and writing programs, it is possible to work from and with a variety of voices to address questions about important principles, and then to consider how to balance principles from inside and outside of the program. This kind of approach also stresses connections between conceptualization—identifying the goals of a project or activity and theorizing those goals—and assessment. This connection speaks to the issue of identifying *issues*—something concrete, something attainable and "measurable" (or, at least, assessable) rather than a problem so vast as to be unmanageable.

The smart organizer—the smart WPA or writing instructor who wants to change stories—will "mix and phase" elements of all three models, drawing on "strategies and techniques from [different] approaches as they go about their work, mixing the strategies and techniques from [different approaches], depending on the needs of the community and the demands of particular projects, and phasing in and out of a particular model depending on the part of the process they find themselves in on a given day" (Fleischer 2000, 83). The key, as Karl Llewellyn's quote implies, is balance. Techniques without ideals, tactics without strategies, actions without principles—a menace. But ideals without techniques, values without tactics, principles without compromise and reality-checking—a mess.

5

TAKING ACTION TO
CHANGE STORIES

> There are upper division writing courses in all disciplines at [my
> institution]. A lot of faculty don't want to teach them because they
> don't have enough assistance and they don't know how to teach the
> courses. For the courses this semester, I decided to offer peer tutors
> to these courses to help with the writing aspects of the course. So
> I'm going to have a class for the peer tutors—they'll get 4 credits for
> taking this class and tutoring in the writing intensive (WI) courses.
> I'm trying to figure out: How can I find students to do it? How can
> I work with their schedules? How can I hook them up with the right
> WI course? What would be most helpful to have in the peer tutoring
> course? How can I work with the peer tutors and the faculty whose
> courses the tutors are placed in?

This anecdote from Larissa, the writing director at a large private
university, illustrates a point made by the Bay Area Organizing
Coalition (BAOC) organizer Eleanor Milroy: "There's a gazillion problems and a gazillion issues" (Milroy 2006). Issues here
might include lack of support for WI courses, reliance on one
faculty member to provide support for these courses, the perception of writing instruction by "content" faculty, and so on.
Using any of the approaches to organizing described in chapter 4, it's easy to imagine how these issues might come to the
fore in discussions with writing program staff, in Larissa's (or
the WPA's) own thinking, or in some combination of both. If
Larissa wanted to tackle one of these issues and work to change
it, a next step would be to develop another frame around the
issue and work to communicate that frame to relevant audiences. To identify this as something separate from organizing
is something of a misnomer, though. The process of shaping

messages helps to identify issues and values, and identifying those issues and values also contributes to the message. As the Opportunity Agenda and Project Strategic Press Information Network (SPIN) put it, "The organizing should drive the [communication] strategy, but communications should always have a place at the planning and decision-making table to help guide the strategic choices of the effort" (Toolkit 2). This chapter will focus on the second part of this equation, developing a communication strategy, as a part of organizing work.

Although it's easy to leap to the assumption that communication begins with developing and broadcasting a message, there are a few steps that are important to take even before that one. First, WPAs and writing instructors need to consider how we are positioned with regard to the issues we want to affect. As discussed in chapter 1, communication theorists make the case that dominant cultural values are reflected in dominant frames and that the narratives extending from these frames reflect and perpetuate those dominant values; as a result, other values linked to other frames are marginalized from the picture. In the case of writing instruction, this means that narratives like the one from the *Chicago Daily Herald* described in chapter 1 are common: students are arriving in college "underprepared"; this underpreparedness is contributing to a general decline in the workforce (and, therefore, the economy); colleges are enrolling students in "remedial" courses that do not constitute real college work; writing is something students learn to do and then do not need additional education on; and so on. Charlotte Ryan suggests that this frame dominance is a form of "sponsorship" (Ryan 1991, 176) that is akin to the literacy sponsorship described by Deborah Brandt. Just as Brandt argued that literacy sponsorship ultimately perpetuates the interests of the sponsors while simultaneously augmenting their ability to shape conceptions of literacy (Brandt 1998, 171–73), frame sponsorship reflects the interests of "multiple social actors" who try to adjust their positions to accommodate challenges and the dominance of their frame (Ryan 1991, 176–77).

What this means for WPAs and writing instructors is that, in many instances, we are up against it—we're trying to reshape frames that have powerful sponsors. Additionally, the analysis in chapters 2 and 3 illustrates that the narratives underscoring these frames are complicated and have the potential to accommodate our own values as well. The analysis in chapter 3 also suggests that WPAs and writing instructors whose perspectives are represented in best practices defined and shaped by professional organizations like the NCTE and WPA are not often in the position of being frame sponsors. However, the analysis of coverage of the SAT writing exam also illustrates that it *is* possible to move into this position through concerted and strategic effort; another piece of good news is that just as there are parallels between some of the strategies for cultivating a base and developing alliances and our own teaching practices, so there are connections between what we do well and the process of shifting frames (and stories) through communication strategies.

Borrowing from WA, SPIN, and others, this chapter offers strategies that writing instructors and WPAs can use to try to affect the frames that surround discussions of writing and writers. These strategies are geared entirely toward affecting frames at the local campus level, because that is where WPAs and writing instructors are likely to have the greatest effect. This focus is consistent with the experiences of MoveOn.org, the IAF, and WA—all of whom stress that frame-shifting is most effective when it is linked with local stories, local examples, and local people. As IAF West Coast Director Larry McNeil puts it, change comes when story is linked with interpretation—without either side of the equation, neither are as powerful (Gustafson 2000, 97).

THE BIG PICTURE

Media and grassroots activists alike agree that there are seven steps involved with (re)framing stories:

- Identifying an issue and a goal for change

- Identifying what we know, and what we need to know, to achieve the goal
- Developing a message
- Identifying audiences for that message
- Crafting specific messages for specific purposes/audiences
- Creating an overall plan to circulate our messages among those audiences
- Assessing our work (Bray 19; Sen 2003, 148–63; Wellstone Action 68–82; Milroy 2006)

Step One: Identifying an Issue and a Goal for Change

As chapter 4 suggests, story-changing work proceeds incrementally. The first step is to identify an issue (not a problem) while simultaneously cultivating a base of supporters and allies with whom to work. What issue we choose to start with also depends on the organizing approach that we use, which in turn also might affect who is included in our base and what allies we make for what purposes. Returning to Larissa's story can illustrate: in an interest-based model, Larissa might not even get as far as identifying any of the items in this list *as* issues because her work on WI courses might begin with relational conversations, and through those conversations she might hear issues that she hadn't previously considered. Here her focus would be identifying issues important to others, bringing together groups to work on these issues, and developing leadership from the groups to continue the organizing effort. Implied here is a connection between addressing issues and long-term change, but long-term change is not an explicit goal.

In a values-based approach, Larissa might have again engaged in organizing conversations, but in and through them identified the values central to her work and the work of the WI faculty in order to identify issues that would advance those values (for instance, the values of writing to learn and the use of writing as a discovery strategy in WI courses). Here, long-term change would always be front and center and the values that any change advanced would be prominently featured in discussions and action. Issues to address through story-changing work, then, would stem from the values at the center of the organizing effort.

In an issue-based approach, Larissa might start from one of the issues listed here—say, lack of support for WI courses—and she might have engaged with organizing conversations with WI faculty to gather information about their perspectives. In those discussions she might have heard that faculty were specifically concerned with class size, for instance, and decided to take on that issue in partnership with the WI faculty as a first step. Each of these models, then, would take Larissa's work as a WPA in a slightly different direction, and each would serve as an important first step in a story-changing process.

Step Two: Conducting a Knowledge Assessment

Once we have identified an issue to tackle, the next step in the story-changing process is to find out what we know about the issue already, and what we need to know. BAOC organizer Eleanor Milroy describes this as a "research action" and notes that these actions both help actors understand "what's going on" and build alliances. If Larissa and her allies identified "class size" as the first issue they wanted to tackle stemming from their concerns about WI courses, for instance, Larissa might address these questions to herself and her colleagues. She might look to institutional research about student performance in WI classes with high enrollments; look to data gathered by her institution (such as the Cooperative Institutional Research Plan [CIRP] or the National Survey of Student Engagement [NSSE]) to find out how entering students feel about their past writing experiences and what they expect to encounter in college and perhaps compare that to national profiles of similar institutions; and talk to WI faculty for specific anecdotes about their experiences teaching WI courses with large numbers of students. Next,

Larissa might look to research in the field on class size, from articles in research journals to position statements such as those on the NCTE Web site (which includes a position on class size) to material on CompFAQ. Then she would need to consider who else was invested in the issue of class size (in changing it, maintaining it, or something else) and why. Along the way, Larissa also might consider how the data she was gathering might be useful, for whom, and why, along with what else she might like to know. All of this research would play a part in the message that Larissa ultimately developed, ideally with her base and her allies, about class size in WI courses.

Activist Rinku Sen summarizes three reasons why conducting this kind of research is so valuable for organizing. First, organizers need solid data to document both the experiences they are representing and the effects of those experiences. Second, data helps to "counteract the opposition's misinformation campaigns." And third, research can serve as the basis for a story-changing publicity campaign (Sen 2003, 116). What *is* the effect on student success of one placement method over another? How *does* using computers in writing classrooms affect students' abilities to, say, achieve the rhetorical analysis outcomes for the course? What effect does one pedagogical approach or another have on students' learning in the course (and how is "learning" being defined)? These are questions that Richard Haswell defines as RAD: "replicable, aggregate, and data supported" (Haswell 2005, 201). During the last year I taught at University of Minnesota General College (GC), I witnessed the power of effective research firsthand. Early in the 1996–97 academic year, then-university President Nils Hasselmo announced that he intended to close GC. Instructional costs were too high, he said; he also pointed to problematic achievement as a motivating factor. But several years earlier, GC had made a strategic decision to give up a tenure line and, instead, hire its own assessment coordinator. During the 1996–97 struggle, the assessment generated by GC was better—more accurate, more thorough, and more rigorously documented—than that provided by the university. GC was able to draw on its own data to refute the university's assertions regarding students. Ultimately, because of these data (and a coordinated effort by the GC to generate lots of what Alinsky called "heat"—protest actions, media coverage, and community gatherings), GC survived. (Unfortunately, although GC thrived between this closure attempt and the early 2000s, it did not make it through the university's next run—it was closed after the 2005–6 academic year.)

STEPS TO HELP IDENTIFY ISSUES AND CONNECT TO VALUES

As a first step toward identifying issues (through a base and working within one of the models described in the previous chapter, or blending elements of all of those models), WPAs or writing instructors might want to consider looking at short-term and long-term goals and then considering connections (or lack thereof) between them:

Short term issues/goalsLong term goals/problems

1.
2.
3.

Once these lists are created it becomes possible to draw lines between them to identify their connections (or lack thereof) to each other. For instance, some sample short-term goals might be to convert the grading scale for a first-year writing class to ABC/no credit and reduce class sizes; a long-term goal might be to change the perception of faculty outside of writing regarding the professionalism and qualifications of writing instructors. While those three goals are connected, they probably aren't directly related and thus might become part of *different* issue campaigns.

KNOWLEDGE ASSESSMENT QUESTIONS

As writing instructors, we work with students to conduct knowledge assessments all the time. In the EMU First Year Writing Program, for instance, students in our first semester

class begin their writing for the term by analyzing what
genres (of reading, writing, viewing, listening, etc.) they
encounter regularly, and what they need to know to participate in those genres. In our second semester research writing class, students reflect on what they know and need to
know to pursue their research. We can also adapt the questions that we use to help students assess their knowledge for
our purposes. We might ask:

> What issue have you identified for story-changing work?
>
> What is your goal regarding this issue?
>
> What do you know about the issue, and from what sources?
>
> At the local level? (e.g., programmatic, institutional, or
> other research [such as the CIRP Freshman Survey, the
> NSSE, or other institutional surveys)
>
> At the national level? (e.g., research in the field;
> CompFAQ; listserv discussions)
>
> How might each of the items that you've identified as
> "knowing" be useful for your goal?
>
> What else do you need to know?
> What's interesting, provocative, or otherwise related to
> your goal or issue?
>
> Who else is invested in this issue?
>
> What is their goal for the issue, and why is it their goal?
>
> What information do they have access to that might be
> useful for you, and why might it be useful?

Step Three: Identifying Audiences/Shaping Messages

As we conduct research to learn what we already know about
the issues we want to affect, we also need to identify the audiences that we want to target for that change-making work. On
the surface, this sounds like a commonsensical assertion—we
help students think about audiences, conventions, and genres

all the time, after all. But as Mike Rose notes, most graduate programs in composition/rhetoric do not offer courses that prepare them for writing or speaking to audiences outside of the field (Rose 2006b, 408).

And there are additional complications to this analysis and development. As discussed in chapter 3, the role of the "public intellectual" that academics have sometimes occupied in communication with audiences outside of academe stems from an analysis of audience that is neither nuanced, flattering, nor accurate. Extending from the technocratic implementation of the progressive pragmatic jeremiad, it implies that the academic is an expert communicating to masses who are unaware of the particulars of the work or situation that we are describing, and thus have little to say about that work. The one-way process of communication (expert→audience) that underscores this approach also contradicts the idea of base development and alliance building that is implicit in all of the organizing models described in chapter 4, and which are essential to changing stories about writing and writers with audiences outside of the field. As one step in this process, then, we need to think about how we position ourselves with regard to audience and message; the approach here suggests that it is crucial that we enact the role of an activist, not a public intellectual, because that role facilitates the kinds of dialogue through which bases are built and alliances developed.

A second challenge associated with identifying audiences and shaping messages stems from the position of the WPA/faculty member in their academic institution. As Richard Miller has pointed out in a variety of articles and books, we exist within a series of large bureaucracies upon which we depend for our livelihoods (e.g., Miller 1998). Our status within these institutions—which itself is influenced by our campus administrators (department heads, deans, provosts)—has profound influences on the kinds of risks that we can take in identifying potential audiences for story changing, and in developing messages to communicate with those audiences. Untenured WPAs, for instance, already have enough at stake. If the audience is an unsympathetic administrator, if the work is not well-received, if the institution does not believe that this kind of work should be rewarded . . . the horror stories that could be played out here are readily apparent. Thus the starting point for discovering those shared values, again, can be the relational conversations described by the IAF that are also at the core of activist intellectualism.

Through these conversations, we might try to learn about the interests and concerns of our potential audiences and link our interests with theirs inasmuch as this is possible, while simultaneously connecting those interests with concerns that those audiences may not have articulated. Redefining Progress (RP) Director Michel Gelobter calls these "big fights" and says that establishing connections between RP's interests and those larger interests is essential.

> [RP takes] what we know a lot about—our expertise area, which in this case is smart economics, the intersection between the economy, social justice issues, and the environment—and make it in service to what I call the "big fights," or the big values issues that are at play in the economy. So—climate change. We know a lot about climate change. That's not a big fight. It seems like everyone cares about it more than anything else, but . . . ask the average person on the street corner [about it, and] . . . it's probably a lot lower than ten other things like their school, their family, the war, the price of gas, stuff like that. So the first step is to see that our issue frame—the way we see the world—is not [everyone's]. The struggle is not to attract more people to us and the way we see the world, but to be of greater service to more people. . . . Take what you know a lot about and put it in service to the big fights where there are lots of bodies and people in motion. (Gelobter 2006)

RP has linked their issue—smart economics—to questions of race and class, for example, arguing that "if the environmental movement is ever going to revive, it must first confront the many ways in which the U.S. has reserved open space for the exclusive use of whites" (Gelobter et al 2005).

Here too is where WPAs and writing instructors can draw on our strengths. The three questions that stand at the center of current discussions about composition, especially in public venues—how should students' literacies be defined; what literacies should composition classes develop, how, and for what purpose; and how should students' literacies be assessed at the end of the class—all extend to larger issues. These include access to education; class, race, and gender issues that are reflected in questions about the value or validity of literacy experiences and manners of expression; and so on (e.g., Heath 1983; Fox 1999; Soliday 2002; Mutnick 1996). In the class size hypothetical that might extend as an issue from Larissa's story, for instance, it would certainly be possible to link the case for smaller class size to student persistence articulated by the hypothetical department head and dean (which in turn links to the need for tuition revenue, addressing the concerns of the vice president for finance). But it might also be possible to extend to another "big fight" not mentioned by these audiences about the "achievement gap" on the campus (if, in fact, there is such a gap and it is of concern to administrators), making the case that smaller classes with more focused instructor attention enables students to form the kinds of mentoring connections cited as one of the single most important factors in student persistence by retention experts (e.g., Tinto 1993).

QUESTIONS TO FACILITATE CONNECTING
TO "BIG POINTS"

WPAs and writing instructors can also turn to strategies that we use on a regular basis to think about audiences for the messages that we develop around issues we want to change, and how our concerns and theirs might coalesce at local and "big" points. ("Rhetorical analysis," after all, is the first category included in the WPA Outcomes Statement.) Adapting heurists for rhetorical analysis to the story-changing process described here, we might begin by reiterating things we already know:

Step one:

What is the issue that you have identified for change?

What is your goal?

Who is included in the base of supporters for this issue? What are their interests?

What do you know about the issue, and from what sources?

What else do you need to know?

Then we might ask questions about the audience for this campaign, their interests, what they believe, and what they know and need to know.

Step two:

Who is the audience for your issue campaign? Who has the power to affect the change you want to see, and what are their interests?

What are the potential "big fights" that your issue might be linked to?

Who is invested in those fights, why are they invested, and what are their positions?

Shaping Messages

While audience analysis can contribute to a story-changing process, we also need to constantly check ourselves as we undertake this analysis and, especially, as we develop messages extending from it. Connecting to big fights may be our strength, but these connections can also lead us quickly into the public intellectual role (and its implication that we know more than others); perhaps more importantly, "connecting the dots" between seemingly distinct ideas is part and parcel of the conventions of academic discourse, but academic discourse is *not* useful for developing or communicating clear messages. It leads straight back to Harris's lament: we are unable to "explain ourselves" to those who do

not share our positions, and part of this inability has to do with
the language we use. We need to keep in mind SPIN's reminder:
"Condense your issues into key messages . . . you do not have to
cover every policy nuance or expound on your social history in
your messages" (Bray 2000, 26).

As a part of the WPA's Network for Media Action (WPA-
NMA), I have both observed and experienced the challenge of
message development. At the NMA workshop held at the 2004
WPA conference, for instance, political consultant Leo Jennings
was facilitating a discussion among 20 or so participants. After a
morning spent learning about media strategies, we were trying
to craft a message that we could use as a central point for a media
campaign about writing and writers. The group was engaged in
a lively and loud discussion about possibilities; Jennings was writing them on the board. Participants offered slogans consisting
of a two dependent clauses joined by a colon (typical of many
titles, including the title of this book), like "Good writing makes
good writers: writing intensive classes contribute to student
persistence." Jennings quickly said, "NO colons!" The workshop
also made it clear that we weren't ready. We had problems, not
issues; we couldn't identify or articulate a position that would
communicate in a clear and coherent way what we were arguing
for; and we didn't have the language to convey the position we
couldn't clearly identify. We also were thinking about operating
at a "national" level (whatever that meant), rather than focusing
on campaigns emerging from local issues.

Jennings and John McDonald, who facilitated the next WPA-
NMA workshop at the 2005 CCCC in San Francisco, conveyed
the same characteristic of an effective message as those identified by WA, with the addition of one characteristic. These messages are:

- clear and concise;
- connect with interests and values of the audience; and
- communicate *our* values and ideas. (Wellstone Action 37)

I would add one characteristic, too: they are conceivable. In other words, people have to "know what we mean." This is the point that Anat Shenker-Osorio makes when she says that progressives need to work out a model of "what [their values] mean or look like" (2006). The idea of conceivable reflects Nunberg's point about narratives, which itself echoes Alinsky's about self-interest—what we want has to become part of the story through which people understand their lives. Media activist Robert Bray recommends using "the brother-in-law test" for our messages—picking someone who isn't "associated with your cause or organization [like a brother-in-law], and see if they understand your issue" (Bray 2000, 16).

Because the work of WPAs and writing instructors is local (tied to our students, on our campuses, in our programs) it is also probably important that our messages are generally locally focused, a point those of us in Jennings's early WPA-NMA workshop hadn't yet understood. While we may want to identify campaigns that we can undertake nationally, it is crucial to recognize that our influence is most powerful on the local level; when we do join together with WPAs across the country we can be most effective if we can bring our experience, base, and allies from the local level to those national conversations so that there is always a clear ebb-and-flow, a dialogue, around how the national concern is of local relevance.

Message Development: Conscious Choice

With these concepts in mind, then, the next step in developing a message is considering the frame for the message. As the analysis in chapters 2 and 3 and the discussion of tactics and framing in chapter 4 suggests, this is a tricky business. On the one hand, the progressive pragmatic narrative that propelled education from the late-nineteenth through the late-twentieth century is quite permeable and has been used by the left and the right. The potential exists, then, for arguments we advance using this frame to undermine some of our individual principles and the collective principles of English instructors/

WPAs as represented by NCTE and WPA. This is what Kent Williamson alluded to when he said that educators have played a role in perpetuating this dominant frame by formulating their concerns within the frame in order to "win" federal and state funding (Williamson 2006). On the other hand, as the interest-based, values-based, and issue-based approaches to organizing described in the previous chapter illustrate, the progressive pragmatic jeremiad also has made possible the kinds of organizing activities that can potentially change the frame around discussions of education. The key, then, is to find a place within this jeremiad that reflects a narrative representing what educators want (and not what they do not want) without incurring strategic losses. Positing arguments that employ different frames means that we run the risk of remaining marginalized from these discussions.

One lesson here is about the importance of conscious choice. Many times, WPAs and writing instructors frame our messages without thinking carefully about how we are doing so, for what purposes, and with what implications. Marguerite Helmers noted a pervasive narrative about what students "lacked" in her analysis of "staffroom interchanges" published in *College Composition and Communication,* for example (Helmers 1994). I would argue that the same narrative is invoked when WPAs justify requests for support for student writing by citing what students cannot do, a strategy not infrequently employed in posts to the WPA-L list.

What's important, then, is to think consciously about developing messages, from the texts themselves to the frames in which they are situated. The four steps described in this chapter and chapter 4 precede this work: 1) identifying an issue (not a problem); 2) assessing what we already know and need to know about this issue; 3) identifying who else is invested in the issue, what are their interests, and what they know about the issue; and 4) identifying the audiences for the message and their interests.

Then, for a moment, we need to put the information we've gathered by working through these four steps aside (but not away) to think about *what we want to say* about the issue. What is the position that we want to advance? This position might represent an agenda developed via relational conversations (in an interest-based approach), one that emerges from our values (in a values-based one), or one that extends from the interests that we have brought to conversations and developed along with others (in an issue-based approach). Note, too, that this step is presented as an affirmative: what we do *not* want to do is articulate what we *don't* want—make clear what we *do* want. One common activity to facilitate this kind of brainstorming is to imagine a campaign with a clear timeline that ends in a headline or a bumper sticker. What would it say? The hypothetical campaign around reducing class size in WI courses extending from Larissa's example might end with a headline like "Writing Intensive Class Sizes Reduced: Students' Grades Rise" or "Faculty Report Better Writing across the Curriculum," for instance. Using this headline as an endpoint, Larissa and her base and allies might then use the backward planning process described in chapter 4, considering what they would need to do, when, and for what purposes to make that headline a reality.

Message Development: Context and Audience

While imagining a headline is a useful strategy for beginning to distill a message, it is only a beginning—really, it's useful primarily as a heuristic for helping us to clarify our goals in one sentence or phrase. The fact is that for WPAs and writing instructors, mainstream media generally aren't the audiences that we'll target for our messages; as much as we might want to affect discussions of writing and writers in those media, our influence is considerably more powerful if we stick to local situations and contexts. In the early days of the WPA-NMA, one participant—a former reporter and editorial board member for one of the nation's largest daily papers—had to remind us that issuing press releases about "our" writing positions would have absolutely no effect other than to add to a journalist's daily collection of trash. On the other hand, local newspapers (campus

and community) have op-ed pages; opinion pieces and letters
to the editor on specific issues certainly can be effective communication pieces. But so, too, can be focused conversations
with audience members; newsletters circulating within our own
programs; articles for other internal newsletters; or events spon-
sored by our programs.

The next step in shaping messages, then, is returning to
the audience analysis and identifying specific audiences for
our messages. Note the possible plural here. It's important
to be able to tailor our messages for different audiences, but
we want to make clear that the heart of the message—what
Rockridge Institute Director Bruce Budner calls the "core
values"—remains consistent (Budner 2006). Of course, this
too is familiar to writing instructors—we work with students to
adapt their communication for different audiences all the time
when we talk with them about analyzing their audience's expectations and making choices about the form, content, style, and
mechanics they will use to meet those expectations.

Another useful tool for helping to craft messages for specific
audiences and take their possible responses into consideration
is a message box. This is a box divided into four quadrants, as
in Figure 3.

FIGURE 3

Our message	Their message
Our response to them	Their response to us

Adapted from Wellstone Action. Used by permission.

To illustrate a message box in action, I'll use an example
from our program at EMU, the shift to guided self-placement
(GSP). While we didn't explicitly rely on the "box" structure,
we developed and anticipated several messages around our core
issues while shifting to GSP. These messages were targeted initially toward the admissions officers and EMU advisors whom we
knew would be instrumental in making the GSP process work;
in creating them, we tried to take into account our rationale for
GSP and the possible obstacles they might see to the process.

FIGURE 4
Admissions/Advising Directors

EMU First Year Writing Program (FYWP) message Students will be more satisfied with their writing course if they make the choice about which course to take themselves.	Administrator/Advising Director message We have little time with students, and need to do things as quickly and efficiently as possible.
Our response to them GSP will take only slightly more time than the previous assessment method, and will result in greater student satisfaction.	Their response to us Writing instructors have little understanding of the realities of student advising.

EMU FYWP message When students feel more in control of their educations, they perform better and are more likely to persist.	Adm./Adv. Director message Standardized test scores are valid representations of students' abilities.
Our response to them Research has demonstrated that there is no correlation between standardized test scores and college success. Students are equally, if not more, successful in writing courses when they make their own choices (e.g., Adams 1993).	Their response to us Writing instructors have little authority to determine valid placement instruments.

EMU FYWP message GSP is a fairer and more effective placement method than what is currently in place (ACT scores).	Adm./Adv. Director message We have little time with students, and need to do things as quickly and efficiently as possible.
Our response to them GSP will take only slightly more time than the previous assessment method, and will result in greater student satisfaction.	Their response to us Writing instructors have little understanding of the realities of student advising.

Developing message boxes like these can be extremely useful. It forces us to create credible, clear and concise, conceivable messages that reflect our values, and also to connect those messages with the interests and values of others. Advisors at my institution, for instance, are invested in student satisfaction for a variety of reasons—for the purposes of retention, for instance, but also because it means that students do not come to them with complaints as often. Similarly, writing instructors in our program wanted to move to GSP because it was more fair, but also because we suspected (rightfully so) that students would be less angry about taking our first semester, elective credit course if they chose to do so, rather than being placed in the course based on a standardized test score. These motivations speak to a range of values—some more idealistic and strategic, some more practical and pragmatic.

Message Development: Media Choice

Once WPAs and writing instructors have shaped messages, the next step is figuring out where and how to communicate them. If the story-changing work in which we are engaged is focused locally and internally, as our work with implementing GSP was, it also makes sense to focus on internal, rather than external, communications—that is, communication pieces that circulate among the audiences who are most affected by the change we want to make. Internal media include things like programmatic newsletters, local Web pages, workshops for relevant audiences, information sheets, and so on—pieces that are directed at specific audiences that do not circulate among broader publics.

Once our allies agreed to the shift to GSP, for instance, we worked with them to develop a communication plan that would facilitate this transition. We identified four communication vehicles to make our points.

Workshops with EMU advisors to help them understand the content of first-year writing classes and the First Year Writing Program (FYWP)'s conceptualization of writers and the work of writing

Articles for the advising center's newsletter explaining the shift to GSP

Handouts for advisors with frequently-asked questions and responses regarding standardized test scores and writing classes

A sheet of talking points for advisors about writing classes
and the GSP process

We also worked with advisors and admissions staff to produce
a brochure containing information about EMU's writing classes,
a survey that students could use for their self-placement, and a
Web site that contained additional information like annotated
assignments and examples of student writing. After each session
where advisors used the materials, we conducted quick assessments asking how the process had gone and whether more or
different information would be useful. In the fall after the first
round of GSP placement (in 2004–5), we held a more extensive
workshop and a lengthy meeting with advisors to review the process; we also developed and distributed an assessment asking students about their experience and satisfaction with the process.
One of the things we learned from this assessment work was that
some students had not considered the GSP brochure as carefully
as we (and the advisors) might have liked; as a result, we developed a letter that would be distributed to parents and guardians
also containing the GSP brochure for the next year's registration
process. The shift to GSP, then, reflected a blend of discussions
with allies and use of strategic internal communications (such as
the advising newsletter, memos, Web sites, and flyers).

Letters to the Editor and Op-Eds
In addition to creating internal communications like workshops, articles, and flyers like the ones that we developed
around GSP, sometimes it can be effective (or just plain satisfying) to try to affect frames around writing and writers by sending editorial columns or letters to the editors of campus and
local newspapers. This seems to be especially true after those
media print a news item that reflects other frames about writing
and writers like the *Chicago Daily Herald* story included in chapter 1. Among the letters I've written to the editor of my local
paper, for instance, are ones reacting to stories about so-called
"remedial" students, students who "cheat" by using the Internet,

and new graduation standards in the state of Michigan. In each of these—as is generally the case with letters to the editor—I was being reactive, not proactive, responding to something in print; among the op-eds I've written for our campus paper, the *Eastern Echo*, is one on why the campus shouldn't renew its subscription to TurnItIn.com. There is more opportunity to be proactive in op-eds, though they are more likely to be published if they are tied to an ongoing story (and thus are also semireactive). These letters and op-ed columns incorporated tips upon which media strategists and news organizations almost universally agree.

- Get to the point. News items are concise and direct, not long-winded and obtuse.

- Link your point to an ongoing story or trend. Media activists note that "three is a trend." As Robert Bray explains, "If you can find three examples of something . . . three examples of discrimination, three points of view that are similar on a particular story—you will position the story for better coverage" (Bray 2000, 17).

- Include specific examples. Community organizers like those included in chapter 4 and media activists alike agree: stories about real people encountering real situations are powerful. This is also another reason why we can be more effective at the local level: if you can localize a national story, you're more likely to get attention from local people (from administrators to journalists).

- Communicate what you *want* to happen, not what you don't want to happen. Remember Lakoff's maxim: when you negate a frame, you reinforce the frame.

- Once you develop your message (and use the "brother-in-law test" to check it), stick to that message. This may mean repeating it more times than you think is necessary, but remember: we're trying to change stories that are dominant in part because people hear them again and again. (Many examples of this kind of repetition can be found with the Bush administration, who are

masters of spin control. "Stay the course," "embolden-
ing the terrorists," and "war on terror" are but a few
examples of the messages that the administration has
stuck to repeatedly to advance their cause.) Media
activist Robert Bray says that "you will know you have
mastered the rule [to repeat your messages] when you
cannot stand hearing yourself repeat your messages
anymore. . . . Every talk you give . . . every interview
you give . . . every letter to the editor you write . . . must
contain your key messages. (Bray 2000, 26)

Some commonsense tips are useful here, too. Whether you're
writing a letter or an op-ed piece, check the news outlet's guide-
lines (which are typically included on the op-ed page). Both letters and op-eds have word limits, and both are subject to editorial
discretion. If they are edited, you won't be consulted about what
is cut or kept, so make sure that your piece says what you want it
to. Use the inverted pyramid style for your piece—put the most
important thing, the message that you want to convey (not the
one you want to negate!) at the beginning, the most important
evidence about that message next, and so on. Make sure that
the least important information about your subject appears at
the end of the piece. If you want to write an op-ed piece, try to
contact the op-ed editor with a query about the piece before
sending. Of course, in major news markets this is not always so
easy; in smaller markets, however, the op-ed editor's address and
phone number is often included in the newspaper. Introduce
yourself, tell her or him what you would like to write about, and
find out whether the paper would welcome such a contribution.
If they would, ask about page limits and deadlines. Op-ed pieces
can be sent to more than one paper; however, you do *not* want
to send them to more than one outlet in the same market. As
with all encounters with journalists, be prepared and polite. This
could be the beginning of an ongoing relationship with this person, and you want to set the right tone.

Cultivating Additional Relationships

In addition to thinking about developing pieces to be printed in media (like letters and op-eds), it is also important to think about how we might cultivate more proactive relationships with media that might allow us to contribute to frames that are used to shape narratives about writers and writing (and education more generally). As with developing alliances around issues that are important to us, this work involves cultivating relationships. In the late 1970s, communication scholar Gaye Tuchman authored an ethnographic study called *Making News: A Story in the Construction of Reality.* Her observations revealed that reporters create a "newsnet," a group of sources to whom they return repeatedly, to construct their stories. A reporter quoted in *Making the News: A Guide for Nonprofits and Activists* makes the same point: "A lot of what gets covered depends on personal relationships at the paper" (quoted in Bray 2000, 39). As the analysis of framing in chapter 4 makes clear, the voices of the dominant culture—"official sources and those holding institutional power" (Ryan, Caragee, and Mainhofer 2001, 180)—are most often present in mainstream media. The perspectives of those (powerful voices) inside the "net" receive greater play; those outside do not. Bray, McDonald, and other media strategists note that "Cultivat[ing] personal relationships with reporters . . . is one of the most important tasks an activist can do when it comes to making news" (Bray 2000, 39; McDonald 2005).

It's important, too, that WPAs and writing instructors be sensitive to the constraints that reporters face in their work if we are to become resources for them. Be aware of cycles and schedules, for instance. If the paper in your community is a morning paper and the story about which you are contacted is not a "breaking" news item, chances are that the reporter will need to have her story in by about four o'clock in the afternoon. If your local paper comes out in the afternoon, most copy is filed by nine o'clock in the morning. Beyond issues like scheduling, remember that the life of a news story is relatively short. If you can link a story that you want to tell to something already going on—that is, if you can find a hook for your story (a national issue, a trend, a scheduled event like the African American Read In or a day devoted to writing, reading, or something else)—it is more likely that media will be interested in the story that you have to tell. And remember issues of simply courtesy: if a reporter calls, return their calls as soon as you can. If they ask you a question to which you do not know the answer, be honest—but tell them that you'll try to learn the answer, or try to point them to someone who can give them the information that they want, as soon as you can. The idea is to become a resource for the reporter, to develop a relationship, not to get your name and ideas in print.

On the other hand, sometimes journalists ask questions designed to elicit particular responses or perpetuate particular frames—questions like, "How do you work with remedial students in your writing classes?" If you think that the label "remedial students" is inaccurate and has implications for education (and your writing classes), you need to think—fast, and on your feet—about how you can reframe that question. Media activist Norman Solomon says that "anyone who's been interviewed very much encounters that problem of being so constrained by the question—I forget who it was that said that the best answer is [to] destroy the question. Given the quality of questions from [some journalists], that would be a pretty darned good idea if you can pull it off without seeming rude or evasive" (Solomon 2006). SPIN's Robert Bray also stresses *responding to questions,* not necessarily *answering* them. He notes that often, in conjunction with his work as an advocate for the rights of gays and lesbians, he was often asked "How many homosexuals are there in America?" Rather than respond with his gut: "How the hell do I know?" Bray says, "I simply responded to the question with my own message, regardless of what the reporter might have wanted to hear. 'No one really knows how many gay and lesbian people there are because we are an invisible minority. But we are found in every community. The real issue is that not one of us should ever be discriminated against or be the victim of violence'" (Bray 2000, 18).

But this is harder than it seems. In a workshop at the WPA summer conference, for instance, two colleagues and I were conducting a workshop on reframing writing through communication with outside audiences. We distributed three scenarios to attendees, all revolving around plagiarism; one group, writing a letter to the editor, began by writing something like, "Although some students do plagiarize, we think this can be stopped." Ouch. Readers need look no further than the first part of that sentence for a headline: "Writing Teachers Speak: Wily and Deceitful Students *Do* Plagiarize!" And the narratives that extend from that statement—about teachers' inability to stop their crafty, technology-savvy, insidious, and duplicitous students from undermining the educational system through the mad downloading of Internet sources—spill right out.

Situations like the ones referenced by Solomon and Bray, where the frame for the question does not reflect the frame that we might want to use, illustrate what media activist Charlotte Ryan calls a "frame contest," an instance when it is clear that the dominant frame is being used repeatedly to frame news about a particular issue. Rather than engage the media in their own game—a strategy which those without equal resources cannot win—Ryan and other activists (e.g., Sen 2003; Bray 2000) suggest shifting the playing field through the creation of news events and alternative vehicles like conferences, reports, or events. Ryan cites a story about Project RIGHT (Rebuild and Improve Grove Hall [a Boston neighborhood] Together), which was concerned that coverage of their neighborhood was framed as "a dangerous place to be avoided. Stories about children falling from windows or being lost, raped, or hit by buses were not inaccurate in isolation, but were inaccurate in their cumulative effects" (1994, 178). A reporter-by-reporter, issue-by-issue approach to shift this narrative wasn't working. So instead, working with Ryan and others at Boston's Media Research and Action Project and the

Boston Association of Black Journalists, Project RIGHT developed and cosponsored

> an educational conference for reporters. . . . Rather than blame reporters for their lack of understanding of the community, a problem exacerbated by the reporters' peripatetic existence, Project RIGHT would provide information that reporters needed, including the community's history and an introduction to the critical issues facing it. . . . By abandoning a responsive approach that focused on criticisms of specific stories, Project RIGHT attempted to reframe itself and its community. (Ryan et al. 2001, 178–79)

NCTE's work around affecting coverage of the SAT writing exam is another example of a frame-shifting event. NCTE's report was carefully timed and strategically released to achieve maximum impact. Like Project RIGHT's conference it was designed to shift the frame—to change the story—about the SAT (and ACT) writing exams; this intention was reflected in everything from the language used to construct the report (accessible, direct, thoroughly researched but not overly academic, and persuasively argued) to the press release that preceded the report's release, to the Web site that was constructed to accompany the report.

Even at the campus level, WPAs and writing instructors can create events that are intended to change stories about writing and writers. The Celebration of Student Writing (CSW), an event held every semester at the conclusion of EMU's second-semester composition course (English 121), is an example of the kind of activity that is well within the purview of our roles as writing instructors and WPAs that can have a powerful effect. For the CSW, students create projects based on their research work in English 121. It begins during the first part of the term, when students identify research interests and questions that are important to them, then conduct observations, interviews, and library research to investigate those questions. Most of the 60–80 sections of English 121 per term incorporate multigenre work—a multigenre research essay, analysis and development of artifacts, or other composition activity that involves more than just creating what my colleague Steve Krause calls "lines on a page." For the CSW, students draw from this work to produce incredible multimedia creations that represent what they have learned, typically accompanied by brief written statements that frame their projects. Every fall, about 700 students participate in the CSW; every winter, about 1,200 students take part. If a section of English 121 decides to participate—and all but a handful do—everyone participates (e.g., Adler-Kassner and Estrem 2003). (For a closer look at the event, visit our CSW Web page at http://writing.emich.edu/fywp/csw and view *Celebration of Student Writing: The Movie* produced by my colleagues Steve Krause and Steve Benninghoff.)

When members of EMU's First Year Writing Program (FYWP) created the CSW, our first thought was that we wanted to put something together to showcase the incredible work students were doing in this course. But we quickly realized that this also would be a powerful way to frame students' writing work *positively*. We wanted the event to be big, loud, and upbeat. We wanted it to showcase what students *could* do, and to create an environment where the only acceptable response to the displays would be "Wow! This is fantastic!" And while there have been a few who have not exhibited this response, the regular assessments that we conduct at or after the CSW tell us that the majority of the roughly 2,500–3,000 participants and visitors yearly who attend one or both of the two CSWs held in the last eight years *have* had this response. Students have told us that they learned at the event that people *are* interested in what they write and, for that reason, feel more interested *in* writing; faculty and administrators who come through tell us that they saw evidence of what students could do.

While the CSW alone has not shifted attitudes about writing and writers on our campus, we know that it—along with our Writing Across the Curriculum (WAC) program, workshops that we conduct for faculty and administrators, efforts like the shift to GSP, and assessment projects that we have undertaken as a

WAC/FYWP group—have contributed to an overall change in the stories told about writers that circulate at EMU. The FYWP and the CSW are now mentioned as highlights of the undergraduate curriculum in the College of Arts and Sciences *Bulletin*, for instance; and an assessment of English 121 was included as one of the pilot projects in EMU's institutional accreditation profile (as part of the Academic Quality Improvement Program [AQIP], a continuous assessment initiative of the Higher Learning Commission of the North Central Association, our accrediting agency). This isn't to say that this shift is permanent, or that we don't hear plenty of discussions of student writing (or student writers) that invoke terms like "don't", "can't," or "won't." But when those discussions do happen, writing faculty are not the only ones in the room saying, "Students in my course have a slightly different experience" or "I think there's another way to think about these questions."

The other advantage of an event like the CSW is that it is within the boundaries of what we can do within institutional bureaucracies. As faculty working for academic institutions, WPAs and writing instructors face a more complicated situation than activists working for nonprofits. Typically, universities *have* spokespeople. They have titles like "director of communications," or "public relations coordinator," and they *also* are trying to affect the ways that stories are framed—especially stories about our institutions. Often, communications directors prefer that we work through them if we want to initiate contact with media beyond contributing an op-ed or a letter to the editor; for example, if you want to attract a reporter to your institution or program for a story, you probably at least want to let the communications director know that you are doing so. That said, you also can work with the communications director to develop hooks that might attract reporters to your institution and program. We can let them know about exciting events that might serve as news hooks like the CSW and share with them stories that might be appealing outside of the campus and help them frame those stories for media. They may not understand our programs or courses, but if they are worth their salt—and most of them are—they understand our universities, and they have good contacts with local media that have been cultivated over a period of years.

Creating an Overall Communication Plan

At the same time WPAs and writing instructors have developed a message (or set of messages) that we want to share with specific audiences, we also need to think about three other questions: Where should these messages be circulated (in internal or external communications? written pieces? spoken pieces?) By whom? When? When EMU shifted to GSP, for instance, the responses to these questions varied at different points in the process, as this chart illustrates.

FIGURE 5

Message	Where	By Whom	When	Audience
Students are more satisfied when they choose their courses	Meetings with admissions/ advising directors	FYWP directors; English department head	Before GSP process initiated	Admissions/ advising directors
Students feel in control if they choose their courses and are more likely to persist	Meetings with advisors	FYWP directors; Admissions/ advising directors	As process is developed	Advising staff
GSP is a more effective and fair means of placement	Articles in advising newsletter	Admissions/ advising directors; FYWP directors	As process is developed	Advising staff

These decisions can be conceptualized using a Gantt chart that lays out the timing of each piece. For instance, given the structure of our admissions and advising system, it would not have been effective to undertake the work in the last box before taking the steps listed before it. The keys to developing a communications plan are to consider several things: What messages should be advanced? When? To whom? Through what means? And for what purposes?

While the example of the GSP messages focuses on a process advanced through a series of offices that are part of EMU's official bureaucracy (which therefore had to go through channels in that bureaucracy), it's also useful to remember that the story-changing process can work outside of official systems. In the teaching practicum for graduate instructors that I typically teach each fall, for instance, we incorporate Field Work Day. It falls near the end of the presemester part of the practicum—when we are meeting all day, every day—and the intent is for graduate instructors to begin hearing about *and formulating responses to* some of the ways that writing and writers are discussed in situations outside of our program. The night before, graduate instructors will read a sampling of some of the many discussions of writers and writing circulating in mainstream media, and a policy report that includes discussion of writers and writing—I have used *Ready or Not,* the report published by Project Achieve/ADP; *Writing and School Reform,* a report published by the National Commission on Writing (which is supported in part by the College Board); and *Crisis at the Core,* a report published by ACT, for instance.

When graduate instructors come in the next morning, we'll talk briefly about their reactions. Then I'll remind them of their charge (which we will have discussed the previous day). They are to go out in pairs for about 90 minutes and find people with whom to talk. They have to tell them that they are teaching first year writing, and then together we brainstorm questions that will give the graduate instructors a sense of how this nonscientific sample perceives college writers and the work of writing instruction. They return to the classroom after their discussions full of information, which they summarize on large sheets of paper and put on the walls of our classroom; then they present their "findings."

Afterward we talk about how we all could, should, and might respond to these statements. What about the associate dean who says that freshman composition is like creative writing? What about the secretary who insists that good writing is writing that is correctly formatted and punctuated? What about the student center worker who says that students can't write? What about the student who said she hated writing until she had a great first year course? Working through these real scenarios and practicing how to respond to them (for good or for ill) helps graduate instructors begin to develop their own senses of how they might participate in this ongoing, larger conversation about writing. And again, there are many links between the activities involved here and the work that we undertake regularly as writing instructors. For instance, on Field Work Day we begin a word/phrase bank that we add to through the term. That is, we list words and phrases that we think are useful for describing what we do so that we can practice using these terms—just as we develop strategies with students regarding a specific writing project so that they can refer back to them later. We also practice talking about the work of teaching writing, just as we design opportunities for students to talk about writing during reader review.

Activities like those involved in Field Work Day also serve to cultivate spokespeople for the writing program *other* than the program directors. As the activists and organizers uniformly mentioned, spreading the work of spreading the word is absolutely crucial—a movement consists of *many* people, not just one. The activities involved in Field Work Day also can help instructors consider how they might involve *their* students in conversations about writing, and perhaps begin to cultivate those conversations. For instance, they also develop word banks in their classes, and sections of English 121 participating in the CSW discuss how they might talk with other students about writing. This kind of planned talking work, too, can be part of an overall communication plan.

In summary, then, a thoughtful communication plan has a series of actions.

- Identify an issue that you want to affect (along with your base and allies)

- Identify what you know through research actions

- Develop a message

- Identify audiences and tailor your message

- Think about where, when, to whom, and for what purposes you will circulate your messages:

    ✦ Internal communications (newsletters, flyers)

    ✦ External communications (letters to the editors, op-ed pieces, press releases through your campus public relations person or directly to media)

    ✦ Meetings

    ✦ Class/pedagogical activities (e.g., Field Work Day, CSW preparations)

    ✦ Events (CSW)

Step Four: Assessing Your Work and Taking the Next Steps

"Assessment" is a word that causes some academics to shake in their shoes. They see it as a Big Brother–like intrusion into their private worlds, a mandate from above that requires them to justify what they are doing for a high-stakes purpose that is usually identified by someone else. But as Brian Huot, Bob Broad, and Patricia Lynne have recently pointed out quite persuasively, assessment is central to our work as teachers. Assessment is also central to the work of the organizing models discussed in chapter 4 (e.g., Chambers and Cowan, Milroy; Gelobter; Wellstone Action; Peterson 2006). It is the process whereby we answer a question that can be deceptively simple: Did it work? Did the story change?

There are several challenges associated with this question, though. First, there's the issue of defining "change," and this has to do with whether we've identified a solvable issue or tackled a bigger picture problem. The example of the SAT writing exam story illustrates this point well: the frame surrounding news stories about the SAT writing exam *did* change as a result of NCTE's organized efforts; however, the writing exam itself persists (and the College Board continues to argue its validity and reliability). In the same way, as a result of activities like the CSW, the shift to GSP, and work on other writing-focused issues on my campus the story that is told about writing and writers has shifted, but that's not to say that some faculty, administrators, students, and others don't still frame their discussions of writing in ways that aren't entirely comfortable for those of us who teach writing.

Thus, the first question that WPAs and writing instructors need to consider when they assess their work is what it will mean to be "successful." Success in the shape of change can be short term. Did the majority of people who attended event X respond in way Y to a question about the event? It can also be long-term. How does population A (students who participated in the CSW) work with subject B (their experience with the CSW and in English 121) over a period of years, and do they link their way of thinking to experience C?

As these questions illustrate, assessing whether a story-changing effort was successful also depends on identifying the audience and context in which "success" is defined. This also refers to the importance of identifying specific audiences and contexts for this story-changing work. The larger the audience—the campus community, the local community, or the public—the more impossible it will be to determine whether a story-changing effort has been successful. It's important to remember, too, that success is necessary for reasons beyond "winning" on an issue—unless people see some payoff for their efforts, they will not likely continue to be active in the cause. This is another reason to keep the focus local. If you identify a specific issue and a specific audience for story-changing work, it's a lot easier to see if and when that work is successful and point to discernable evidence of a "victory." True, there will be other stories to change—and people will be more excited to engage in that work when they see that they can, in fact, have some effect.

These potentially complicating issues point to two things: the importance of developing a clear and straightforward plan to change stories (starting with identifying an issue and working through all of the steps described in this chapter); and considering the assessment of that plan as it is being developed. What will be the purpose of the assessment? The most straightforward response would be to figure out if the story-changing effort was successful. Who will be the audience? Again, the simplest response is "we are," the group who is trying to affect the change. Finally, how will you know if you have been successful? The headlining-brainstorm exercise described earlier can help with this—did you get the headline you wanted to? Did you achieve the result? If you did, what worked—what went right, what lessons can you learn, what can you take away from the experience to use again? If you didn't, what didn't work—what could you and others have done differently, what might have been more successful, what can you use to rethink your strategy?

CONCLUSION: CHANGING STORIES

The steps outlined here, from identifying an issue through assessing work on that issue, overlap with the process of developing a base and forming alliances described in the previous chapter. The three organizing models there—interest-based organizing, values-based organizing, and issue-based organizing—provide structures through which WPAs and writing instructors can consider some of the questions that arise in the process of identifying issues and audiences, identifying and defining messages, formulating a communication plan, and assessing the work of the story-changing effort. Through an interest-based model, work is tactical. Issues arise from conversations with interested and invested individuals; alliances are formed that can result in victories on those issues; audiences and messages are shaped by the base and allies that reflect their goals with regard to the identified issues. Success is achieved when the issue is won—when the job program is funded, when class sizes for WI courses are reduced. These issues are relatively easy to see; their solutions are easily observed. The alliances around them might be short-term or may result in longer relationships, but their endurance is not the primary concern; instead, the objective is to achieve victory on the issue and to identify leaders who might help to identify other issues and lead to the development of other alliances in the process.

Through a values-based model, work is strategic. A base forms around shared values, and alliances are developed with others who share those values. The base and allies identify issues that arise from their set of shared values, and the messages designed to change stories about those issues always have the values of the base and allies in mind. Successful story-changing work means that the frame is changed—the values of the base and allies are evidence in discussions about the issue. Stories about the SAT writing exam that lead with and are dominated by questions raised by the NCTE, coverage of the Iraq war dominated by strains on the troops and not successes in the field, discussions about WI courses that focus on how central administration can facilitate writing-to-learn—are all evidence of values-based victories. These issues are bigger-picture and longer term. While the base and alliances identified through them are likely to be more enduring, identifying whether a victory has been achieved or not is less clear than through an interest-based model because the conception of "winning" is less clear (what does it mean to shift the values around an issue?); because the assessment methodologies are more complicated (content analysis of news coverage of a specific issue, for instance); and because it can be challenging to point to specific evidence of gain in the short term.

An issue-based model blends elements of interest- and values-based organizing. It starts with individuals' interests and works outward to their values, targeting long-term change through short-term projects. "Winning" through an issue-based model would include tactical gains—victories on specific issues, and would then extend to the kind of longer-term values shifting that is the core of values-based organizing. This is the kind of shift, for instance, that seemed to be taking place around No Child Left Behind (NCLB) in March 2007. An increasing number of individuals (such as Democratic Senator Charles Schumer of New York) and organizations (such as NCTE) are critiquing the foundations of NCLB (including the funding appropriated for it and the research studies used to support it), and Congress is beginning to look closely at its design and operation. Tactical actions, like the focused critique of the work of the National Reading Panel and the reading research underscoring Reading First (discussed in chapter 1) seems to be leading to strategic shifts.

Ideals with strategies; strategies with ideals—these are the keys to changing the stories that shape the work that we do as WPAs and writing instructors. There will always be much that we want to change, of course, because there will always be people (and organizations) who decry students' preparations, or what's happening in classrooms, or other aspects of education that are important for us. But we can have some influence on how these discussions take place and how they are framed if we work strategically. We can think about where we have the most influence and the loudest voices—at our local levels. We can think about who we can reach out to, learn from, and enlist as allies. And with them, we can develop a communication plan that helps all of us shape and communicate messages about writers and writing to audiences who might just attend to those messages—and change the stories that they tell.

6

WORKING FROM MY OWN POINTS OF PRINCIPLE
Tikkun Olam, Prophetic Pragmatism, and Writing Program Administration

We all know this story: "I was chatting with someone in/on <insert location here—airplane, airport, grocery store line, child's school, etc.>, and the conversation turned to what we did for a living. When I said that I taught writing, the person said <insert negative comment about writers or writing here— 'Oh! I'd better watch my grammar around you!'; 'Don't you find today that kids can't write?'; 'Don't you find that kids watch too much TV/play too many video games/interact with media I don't know to the detriment of their writing skills?'>."

We've heard this tale (at conferences, in professional publications, perhaps at our own institutions), and perhaps we've even participated in conversations that extend from it. Here's one example. For the last three years, I've worked as a writing tutor at an organization whose mission is to provide writing workshops and tutoring for students in southeastern Michigan. I also help to train other writing tutors; every other month or so, they come to talk about their expectations and learn about working with the kids who come in daily after school. Sometimes in these conversations a tutor trainee will make a disparaging remark about "student writing"—not, typically, the writing of a particular student, but student writing generally. Of course, we discuss the comment in the context of our work, focusing especially on the fact that students are coming for help with their work (including writing), and that a key point of providing that help is being encouraging, supportive, and optimistic. Once we move beyond this general lament to specific instances, the issue becomes more complicated yet less prominent among future tutors' concerns.

This story about students and writing—that students can't write, that communications media are interfering with language development—extend from the progressive pragmatic jeremiad discussed in chapters 2 and 3 of this book. Underscoring this story is the idea that the purpose of schooling is to impart in students (via the stewardly and technocratic approach) the critical intelligence that they need to develop methods to overcome the obstacles facing the nation. Language use is inexorably bound up with the development and demonstration of these methods, and evidence that language is being used "correctly," in a way that demonstrates achievement, is understood to be manifested in things like "proper grammar."

At the same time, here in the dawn of the twenty-first century we Americans are experiencing the same kind of communications revolution that occurred at the beginning of the twentieth; a dizzying array of communications (from video games to the Internet to the ever-increasing capacity of cell phones) are changing boundaries of space and time just as railroads and the development of the motion picture industry and radio did at the beginning of the last century. And just as dominant cultural groups reacted to the development of those media (by using them for the purpose of spreading their own messages, or by protesting against them, or by removing themselves from the arenas where those media were widely used), so the same is happening today, as is demonstrated in comments about how these media must interfere in negative ways with the development of students' critical intelligences.

Contrast this story with another. For the last two years, I've been involved with making a film *Who Is a Writer?: What Writers Tell Us*. This film is part of a larger WPA Network for Media Action project called the National Conversation on Writing. For it, composition instructors, students, and anyone else who read the call for videographers interviewed virtually anyone we could find to interview. Rather than focusing on student writing, the questions for these interviews focused on the interviewee's *own* writing. The first question was, "Are you a writer?"

Other questions asked interviewees to talk about their most and least positive writing experiences, about what helped them and didn't help them write, and so on. And not surprisingly, the stories in this film are quite different than the ones told by the people who come for tutor training. People say things like, "I'm a good writer when I'm working on things I like to write, but I'm not a good writer when I'm not working on things I like." Students talk about writing poetry and putting together raps. One of my favorite clips comes from a teenager who says that he doesn't think of himself as an especially good writer, but that he likes to write things with "simple sentences—kind of like Hemingway" (Vandenberg).

This film captures very different stories about writers than the ones described at the beginning of this chapter. The methodologies used to elicit these different tales also speak to the implications of some of the strategies for changing stories discussed in this book. In the first instance, the narratives focus on "students" and "writing," casting these ideas within a dominant narrative about writers and writing that is currently circulating outside of our profession. It is reflected in news stories like the one from the *Chicago Daily Herald* that I cited in chapter 1; it is located in *A Test of Leadership*, the report from the Spellings Commission on Higher Education, as well as in *Ready or Not* (from the American Diploma Project) and in policy documents and studies (like those produced by ACT) discussed in chapter 3. In this narrative, students are failing. They don't know, they can't do, and things aren't good. It also suggests that teachers, by extension, are struggling; they aren't teaching students what they need to know. As a result, students are not developing the critical intelligence necessary to contribute to the nation's progress toward achievement of the virtuous democracy, a belief that is encompassed in statements about how America is not educating workers for the twenty-first century (and, as a result, is losing its competitive edge). The frame surrounding this narrative is very tight and brooks few challenges, as the discussion framing in chapter 1 suggests. Linguistic researchers and frame analysts

like Anat Shenker-Osorio and Real Reason note that this frame
also can be reinforced when discussions focus on abstract categories, like "writers" or "students," because these do not refer
to specific individuals (Shenker-Osorio 2006). The result, then,
are stories about *writers, teachers, education*—but not any specific
writer, teacher, or school.

The vignette about *Who Is a Writer?* tells a different story. It
is about how people—actual students, teachers, others—feel
about their own writing. They talk about when they feel com-
petent as writers and when they do not, about how they know
when they have done a good job with writing and when they
have not; about when writing has mattered or not mattered, and
what difference that investment has made to them. The frame
here is less tight, in part because it is more complicated. It suggests that qualities of good writing are context- and situation-
specific—sometimes people write some things well, and others
not as well. The job of teachers, then, is different. It might be to
help writers identify their strengths, examine what they already
know to do those things better, and consider how they can build
on and transfer those things they do well to new writing situations and challenges. The questions used to elicit this narrative
are a bit different as well, because they focus on specifics—on
real individuals (the interviewees, actual people whom they
know) and on real writing situations.

Just as these examples capture two different stories about
writers, this book has examined a number of stories that run
through and influence the work of writing instruction and writing program administration. These stories are centered in three
questions: what literacies students have when they enter the academy; what they should learn in writing classes (and who should
determine what they learn); and how their literacies should
be assessed once those classes are completed. In the dominant
frame surrounding these stories, contemporary education does
not come out looking particularly effective. These stories say
that students do not know what they need to know coming out
of high school, and that once they enter college, instructors

don't understand what students need to know and do to participate in twenty-first-century democracy, so other experts (ADP,
ACT, or others) must step in both to develop curriculum and
design assessments to make sure that students are learning what
they should. These stories are told in policy reports and in news
stories (that are themselves often influenced by those same
policy reports). They are also repeated in the kinds of everyday
dialogues that people have about writing.

COLLAPSING THE TELESCOPE: FROM SOCIAL PRACTICES TO PERSONAL PRINCIPLES

The quote from Karl Llewellyn that I invoked in chapter 1,
"strategies without ideals is a menace, but ideals without strategies is a mess [*sic*]," summarizes the challenge faced by WPAs
and writing instructors who want to change this dominant
frame and the stories extending from it. In that chapter I also
discussed the telescoping process described by Robert Coles,
organizers associated with the IAF, and others who discuss the
extension from personal principles and passions to broader
social concerns. These personal stories are always with us. They
are at the core of the "undivided self" mentioned by Palmer;
the "present" teacher that O'Reilley writes about; the "lived
experience" and its connection to classroom work described by
Ronald and Roskelley; and the broader extensions of "personal
faith" that Elizabeth Vander Lei discusses (2005, 6–8). These
are our personal "effective ideals" and "moral compass[es]"
(Rodgers 52). And just as they are motivational for us, so they
are for others. Working from our own stories, learning about
and connecting with the personal stories of others—this is the
beginning point for building the kinds of alliances that are at
the core of the story-changing work described by the community organizers and activists cited in chapters 4 and 5, the kind
of story-changing work that might be represented by projects
like *Who Is a Writer?*

As part of the discussion of personal principles in chapter
1, I also mentioned some of the my own personal stories about

experiences as a middle and high school student, stories that I locate at the core of my ideals. Because of the way I understood my (often terrible) performance, I didn't feel like I was good enough. In college, my self-perception began to shift, and after a surprising (to me) return to graduate school after a few years I began to connect experiences like mine to broader issues and to systematically study definitions of literacies and the ideologies and contexts that they reflected and perpetuated. Through this process, and as I've continued to teach and administer writing programs, these lived experiences have continued to contribute to ideas at the center of my work and life. These are the mantras by which I live as a teacher. Value students, their ideas, and their writing. Never, never, never make someone feel as if they can't do something. Treat everyone enthusiastically and in open and welcoming ways; work from what writers *bring*, not what they *do not bring*, to a class or a writing program. Care about people. Listen, and listen some more, to hear what they have to say and not what you think about what they have to say. Advocate for writers and writing, and also help writers and teachers develop strategies to do the same thing for themselves. Be smart and try to understand things from as many perspectives as possible. At the same time, form alliances and try to use those as a basis from which to develop shared values that then extend to messages through which we communicate our ideas to others. These experiences serve as the starting point for my own telescope, the small end of "personal stories."

PERSONAL PRINCIPLES: TIKKUN OLAM AND PROPHETIC PRAGMATISM

As I consider connections between my personal stories and these mantras, I see them reflected in two principles that guide my work as a teacher and a WPA: the idea of *tikkun olam* as I enact it through the practice of secular humanistic Judaism, and the notion of prophetic pragmatism. While I hardly would suggest that these principles should underscore others' work, I will explain them and their connections to my own practices. I do so not because I feel that these are representative or more virtuous than other principles, but to both share and model the kind of thinking that I have done about this telescoping process from personal to social that is at the heart of the change-making processes described here.

Tikkun Olam: Transforming the World

Within Judaic literature, there are a number of definitions of *tikkun olam,* each of which invests the term with slightly different meanings. The idea of *tikkun olam* originates from Kabbalah, a mystical Jewish tradition. In that version, God consists of (and is contained in) a series of vessels. According to Rabbi Irwin Kula, one account of this story says that:

> When God contracted, the vessels shattered from the incredible energy and force, and shards were scattered throughout the universe. Each of these fragments contained a spark of light, a grain of God. . . . [Luria] taught that humankind could heal the Divine, restore God through contemplative practice such as study, prayer, and meditation, and through acts of loving kindness. If humankind can gather the shards of good and evil, love and hate, destruction and creativity, we can release the sacred sparks within them, dissolve all dualities, and repair all that is. We can make God whole again. This Kaballistic call to repair the world by making it whole is called tikkun olam. (Kula 2006, 295–96)

Having laid out this version, it's important to note that discussion (and debate) about the interpretation and application of germinal texts, experiences, and laws (such as this description of tikkun olam) is a central part of Jewish cultural practice. Thus, extending from this definition (which I am confident that some Jews would argue is not the most influential conception of the term), tikkun olam has been variously defined as "repairing the world," "restoring the world," or "healing and transforming the world."

As a humanistic Jew, I prefer (and work from) definitions that tend toward "transforming" because they reflect an epistemology that is consistent with my beliefs.[1] In this conception, these actions are directed toward the benefits of those on earth and necessitate negotiating the messiness of difference, of diversity, in the here and now (rather than trying to smooth out that diversity). Engaging in *tikkun olam* will help elucidate what Kula calls the "magnificent kaleidoscope of our many selves. . . . There is no cohesive self awaiting our discovery; no world waiting to be redeemed. There is no unity behind the curtain. The mystical realization that awaits us is not a leap into Oneness but a soaring into solidarity with and empathy for the world's multiplicities" (297, 300). This interpretation resonates with me and reflects the ways in which I work to enact *tikkun olam*.

Just as there are multiple definitions of *tikkun olam*, there are also different ideas about how to enact the principle within Jewish culture. But the discussion and debate around this enactment is a central part *of* Jewish culture and, in its way, its own act of *tikkun olam*. The value of debate and discussion is represented in a story about Rabbi Hillel, one of the foundational philosophers of Judaism. A non-Jew approaches Hillel and challenges him to define Judaism's essence while standing on one foot. "What is hateful unto you do not do unto your neighbor," Hillel says. "The rest is commentary—now go and study" (Telushkin 1991, 112). Most forms of Judaism don't provide interpretations; they provide opportunities for meditation and discussion. The value of study and discussion is also represented in the Talmud (which literally means "study"), a document used by observant Jews as a basis for their discussions of Torah (the first five books of the Hebrew Bible). Accumulated over centuries of rabbinic interpretation, Talmudic historian Robert Goldenberg explains that the Talmud represents a series of conversations, rather than a set of answers. "Talmudic conversation," he writes, is like "a gathering where everyone is talking at once" (Goldenberg 156). The primary purpose of the text (each page of which is so packed with discussion that it looks like a Hebrew version of a nineteenth-century newspaper) is to preserve the thinking of earlier generations and provide a structure for ongoing discussion.

My own conception of *tikkun olam*, tinged with secular over-
tones and an emphasis on dialogue, reflects Kula's conception
that the principle concerns "mend[ing] the disharmonies of
the world through the pursuit of social justice" (Kula 2006,
296). This instantiation of the principle also resonates with
the concept of prophetic pragmatism outlined by Cornel West.
Pragmatism, especially as it has been enacted through progressive ideologies, has provided a rich and diverse culture through
which efforts to educate American citizens have developed.
Prophetic pragmatism, the twentieth- and twenty-first-century
manifestation of this philosophy, is predicated on three elements: profound faith in and advocacy for the power of individuals to make a difference and improve democracy, balanced
with acknowledgement that both these efforts and the democracy is situated in and shot through with differences in power
(West 1989, 227); the importance of processes intended to
forward the possibility of "human progress" that acknowledge
and attempt to address profound differences in power among
citizens, coupled with "the human impossibility of paradise"
(229); and an acknowledgement that process is predicated on
the adaptation of old and new traditions to "promote innovation and resistance for the aims of enhancing individuality and
promoting democracy" (230).

While the principles of *tikkun olam* and prophetic pragmatism may seem divergent, in fact they are closely aligned. There
are three core elements that are shared among both. First is that
this work is grounded in action in the here and now. Menachem
Mark Kellner notes that Judaism generally "emphasizes human
behavior over general claims of theology and faith" (Kellner
1995, 13). In this sense, its detractors refer to it as "a religion
of pots and pans" because its central concerns have to do with
day-to-day living, what Harold Schuweis calls "this worldly"
behavior (as opposed to "otherworldly" action) (Schuweis 29).
Jewish activist and economist Bernardo Kliksberg notes that
this emphasis on action is a "unique feature" of the culture
(Kliksberg 2003, xii). As Kula puts it, "Jewish wisdom teaches

that nothing is more important than what we do. Being paralyzed by indecision is not an option. It's incumbent upon every human being to contribute to the world, to make a difference. That's why our decisions are so important, why as many angles or paths as possible should be considered" (Kula 2006, 94). Rabbi Richard J. Israel also reflects on the call to act when he says that he must "live a life of commitment plagued by great doubts. I must act without hesitancy out of information that is questionable" (Israel 1995, 124). The focus is always on action in the present moment.

The principle of present action is also deeply embedded in prophetic pragmatism. As Cornel West explains, this approach affirms the "strenuous mood" that is embedded in pragmatism, especially its proclivity for action in the here and now. This principle was initially articulated by William James in his germinal essay "What Pragmatism Is." In that piece, James uses a story about a squirrel circling a tree as a metaphor for the kind of present-moment thinking essential for pragmatic action. James explains that, returning from a hike during a camping trip, he found his companions in a "ferocious metaphysical dispute. . . . The *corpus* of the discussion was . . . a live squirrel supposed to be clinging to one side of a tree-trunk; while over against the tree's opposite side a human being was imagined to stand" (James 1910b, 43). The human tries to see the squirrel, the squirrel avoids being seen by circling the tree. The question: does the man go around the squirrel, or the squirrel around the man? James's response, ultimately, was that it didn't much matter which animal went around which; that, in fact, the only debates of consequence were ones that *had* consequence for actions in the here and now. As James later explains,

There can be no difference anywhere that doesn't make a difference elsewhere—no difference in abstract truth that doesn't express itself in a difference of concrete fact and in conduct consequent upon that fact, imposed on somebody, somehow, somewhere, and somewhen. The whole function of philosophy ought to be to find out what definite difference it will make to you and me, at definite instants of our life, if this world-formula or that world-formula be the true one. (James 50)

While James was not especially concerned with here and now action directed toward broader social change, the idea of focusing on present action as it is articulated in his work has been infused, in prophetic pragmatism, with concerns about material and social realities. As West explains, prophetic pragmatism "never giv[es] up on new possibilities for human agency—both individual and collective—in the present" (West 1989, 228).

In addition to a focus on action in the here and now, both *tikkun olam* and prophetic pragmatism reflect a compulsion to combine action and reflection. Rabbi Richard Israel explains that the Bible is not a "rule book," not a "source of values [but] a decoration to give apparent substance to the values we already have" (Israel 1995, 124, 119). It's what Jews *do* with this information, with the interpretations that stem from the Bible, that have more influence. But even that tradition does not dictate action, Israel says. It is "a check on and a source of social values . . . a goad, a guide, and a goal: a goad, in that it prods us into caring; a guide, in that it presents us with some limitations and suggested lines of action; a goal, in that it gives us a vision of [an] ideal future" (124). Jewish tradition and culture provides Jews with texts and traditions that can be used for reflection; that reflection, in turn, is a central part of the process of discovery that is the core of the practice. This is the point of Kula's definition of *tikkun olam*, in fact. He's making the case that acts in the name of *tikkun olam* are represented in ongoing processes—they are gerunds ("ings," verbal nouns), not static nouns. The act is in the *doing*, not in the *having done*. "The truth *can* set us free," Kula writes, "but only if we're always in the process of discovering it" (Kula 2006, 3, emphasis in original). This discovery is predicated on intentional action—the kind of action that we might call reflexive.

In the same way, prophetic pragmatism places a high premium on self-awareness and situated action. Raymond Williams describes this element of reflexivity:

> We have to see the evil and the suffering, in the factual disorder that makes revolution necessary, and in the disordered struggle against the disorder. We have to recognize this suffering in a close and immediate experience, and not cover it with names. But we follow the whole action: not only the evil, but the men who have fought against evil; not only the crisis, but the energy released by it, the spirit learned in it. We make the connections . . . and what we learn in suffering is again revolution, because we acknowledge others as [human]. (quoted in West 1989, 229)

The final element at the core of this thought is the notion of communal dialogue, since it is this dialogue that fuels the kind of reflective and reflexive examination described above. Given the fact that Jews were largely segregated from mainstream cultures (in shtetls, ghettos, and other communities) until the late eighteenth century, often through legal and political strategies that systematically robbed Jews of economic and human rights, it is perhaps not surprising that Jews found (and continue to find) strength in community. Extending from this position, Daniel J. Elazar argues that Jews engage in a politics that is "multifaceted and dialectic, . . . a continuing dialogue based upon a shared set of fundamental questions" (Elazar 1997, xix). This tradition is rooted in the Bible, but it is "filtered through the Talmud" and has found expression throughout Jewish history (xx). Laurie Zoloth-Dorfman, a Jewish ethicist, makes the case that "the way to the truth of an action" in Jewish decision making is through this dialogue and the "shared narrative" that develops from it. "If we are to develop new language beyond individual entitlements," she argues, "it must be language rooted in story and community that draws from a method that is itself dialogic and communal" (Zoloth-Dorfman 220). Marshall J. Breger, too, emphasizes the importance of communal dialogue. "The quest for spiritual meaning [in Judaism] has never been primarily a

persona confession for the lonely man of faith. . . . The Judaic
conception of a meaningful spiritual life is communal in orientation" (Breger 2003, 2). In other words, work through dialogue
to develop processes, methods, and strategies is used to discuss,
refine, defend, and advance ideals that are central to the community (e.g., Elazar 1997).

Again, this notion of dialogue and dialectical action also
is embedded in prophetic pragmatism. It stems in part from
pragmatism's evolution from America's foundational narrative discussed in chapter 2. In that narrative, America is always
progressing toward the achievement of a virtuous democracy.
Along the way, though, obstacles crop up that impede this progress. They are overcome when like-minded individuals have the
liberty to come together and, in and through dialogue, develop
processes and methods by which to overcome them. The dialogue that is generated toward these solutions and the solutions
themselves, in fact, are also important elements of advancing
the nation's progress; without them, the "natural" evolution of
American ideals would not occur.

Participatory dialogue directed toward the development of
processes and methods for overcoming obstacles is also a central part of pragmatism. This emphasis on dialogue—on *communication*—runs throughout John Dewey's work, for instance.
Communication theorist James Carey locates in that work a
"ritual" perspective where communication "comprises the ambi-
ence of human existence [and where] . . . reality is brought into
existence, is produced, by communication—by .. . the construction, apprehension, and utilization of symbolic forms" (Carey
1989, 24–25). One of the primary concerns of Dewey's work
was focusing Americans' prodigious inclinations for dialogue
toward "democratic" ends; that is, toward the development of
a culture that embodies "the best of American democracy" and
perpetuates the "march" of that democracy toward a more fully
developed achievement of it (West 1989, 71).

Connection between larger principles and everyday actions,
enacted through reflective and reflexive practice, formulated in

dialogue among community—these are central to the practices of *tikkun olam* and prophetic pragmatism as I understand and try to enact them. The "ground rules for action" formulated by Rabbi Richard J. Israel—ground rules that almost directly echo principles framing the work of organizers whose work is discussed in chapters 4 and 5—make sense to me in this regard: "Fight for things that matter; choose areas in which you can be effective— reduce problems to a size that you can comprehend and do something about; occasionally, pick areas where you have a choice for success; [and] understand your opponents" (Israel 1995, 127).

Certainly, those more knowledgeable about Jewish culture, history, ethics, and values might frame *tikkun olam* differently; to be sure, given the propensity for debate and discussion in Judaism, there are arguments to be raised around my framing of this work. And I am not entirely comfortable with this explanation of the practice because, as a reflective and reflexive thinker, I know I've missed a lot. But then again, not knowing, questioning, reflecting, debating—these are all central characteristic of Judaism and the principle of *tikkun olam*. As Kula notes, "The yearning for Truth and Enlightenment is one of our defining human qualities. We can seek with passion and commitment while knowing we'll never get there. . . . Jewish wisdom sanctions the yearning, even ennobles it, at the same time teaching that there is no meaning; only a kind of dance between meaning and ambiguity; understanding and misunderstanding; faith and doubt; essence and no-essence" (Kula 2006, 14, 42). The challenges that I face—as a person, a parent, a spouse, a WPA—is to figure out, in new ways every day, not just how to enact principles that inform my practice (like *tikkun olam*), but what those principles mean as I enact them and how that meaning changes.

TIKKUN OLAM, PROPHETIC PRAGMATISM, AND CHANGING STORIES

The idea for this book came to me in a flash as I was sitting in a restaurant after a day at the 2004 NCTE conference. Two friends and I were bemoaning the left's seeming inability to make a dent in the powerful frames that were being advanced by the right around everything from the Iraq war to education. I said, "I'm going to learn what they do, and I'm going to figure out how we can use those strategies, too."

If that need seemed compelling in 2004, it seems even more so in 2007. As noted earlier, the stories that circulate about students and teachers repeatedly are not often echoed in research from the field, in statements and studies from professional organizations, or by individuals telling stories about themselves as writers. But frustratingly, educators sometimes seem unable to combine strategies and ideals to change these stories by shifting the frames from which they extend. Throughout this book I have cited examples of this conundrum and its possible consequences, but I must invoke one more. This comes from opening remarks delivered by Sarah Martinez Tucker, undersecretary for higher education, at a regional hearing on the Education Department's (ED's) Spellings Commission Report, *A Test of Leadership*, in June 2007, a hearing intended (in Tucker's words) to help attendees develop "local ownership" of the ED's "national agenda . . . so that more Americans have access to opportunity" (Tucker 2007). Tucker went on to say that in her position as undersecretary, "it's almost like I'm sitting in this position and responsible to ensure that all Americans have access—but I feel like I'm watching a train wreck. . . . We debate whether we're broken, but as a system we're not producing enough Americans with post-secondary credentials. We will put ourselves in a position where the country is not economically viable" (Tucker 2007). Not surprisingly (given that she was a Spellings Commission member, and now a Bush administration official), Tucker's remarks provided additional support for the frame surrounding and narrative advanced in *A Test of Leadership*: higher education isn't doing a good enough job maintaining the progressive pragmatic jeremiad discussed in chapter 2; teachers are not developing students' critical intelligences in ways that prepare them for participation in twenty-first-century democracy; and the country will surely falter if something is not done.

As a writing instructor and a WPA, I've long thought about how we can take action to change stories like the one that is reflected in Tucker's remarks. This is a long-dominant narrative, and one that many other compositionists (and literacy educators) have attempted to shift as well. Here I've tried to adapt strategies from organizers and activists from outside of our field for this purpose, thinking about how we can use ideas about building relationships, developing and disseminating messages, and engaging in other positively based work to change frames around writers and writing instruction. But in and through the principles of *tikkun olam* and prophetic pragmatism, I also continually ask questions about this work. One that I ask myself— and which has been raised by others (e.g., Hesse 2001)—has to do with the fact that in it, I *am* advocating for particular ideas, stances, and approaches. In this book, in fact, I am both telling stories and invoking the idea of stories, tropes, and frames to advance different kinds of stories. Clearly I have some strong beliefs about the ways that writing instruction and the work of writing instructors and WPAs *should* and *should not* be framed. I think that many WPAs and writing instructors *do* understand how to prepare students for participation in the democracy; at the same time, I don't always agree with the definition *of* that democracy as it is shaped in documents like *Ready or Not.* That is, I believe—like Saul Alinksy, Ernesto Cortes, Rinku Sen, MoveOn.org, Wellstone Action, the SPIN Project, Norman Solomon, the other activists and organizers cited here and many others—that citizens are prepared to participate in the democracy when they have the critical intelligences to assess the social and material conditions that currently exist and make conscious decisions about how to improve those social and material conditions for the greatest number of people. In education, this can be cultivated through the development of what Jay Robinson calls "civic literacy," a process enacted when students (with their teachers) are invited to consider the contexts and implications of their actions, especially as they are enacted through language (Robinson 1998).

But does this perspective jibe with the notion of engaging in dialogue, of listening, of making alliances between my own ideas and those of others? That's a question that I wrestle with every day as I try to consider how best to enact ethical, meaningful, and valid work in the writing program that I administer and in my own classes. I hope that my principles also guide this wrestling, as through them I try—*try*—to be respectful of divergent positions. I will say this, too. I have found that the strategies I have learned about through this research extremely helpful. People with whom I work—administrators on my campus, students in our classes, colleagues in my department—share a deep and passionate commitment to student learning, and that passion is motivated from stories of their own. Finding these and listening to them, I have found that we share some common goals, and we can work from these goals in what I hope are meaningful and productive ways. This, then, is my individual response.

As a professional in the field, I'll say this. If individual WPAs and writing instructors are comfortable with current responses to questions about what literacies students bring to our classes, about how those literacies should be developed, and about how they should be assessed, then we need not worry about the future of our writing programs and courses. However, if WPAs and writing instructors are not comfortable with the current direction that discussions about education (and writers and writing) are taking, it is important for us to be able to think and act strategically to change the frames around those discussions and the stories emanating from them. I've suggested here that these strategic actions should start with and proceed from principle, whatever that principle is for instructors and programs. To me, the central principles of Judaism that are bound up in *tikkun olam* and prophetic pragmatism—action and reflection that is grounded in the present moment enacted as a result of and through communal dialogue—suggest different ways of going about this reframing work. From the moment I entered a classroom, I have been unwilling to frame my courses (or, in some cases, our writing program) as ones that are designed to address some perceived "need"—or, as is more often invoked, some "lack"—that students bring with them to college, a stance that doubtless comes from my own experience as a student who felt myself "lacking." Instead it's been important for me to think about what students *have*, what they *bring*, what they *can* do, and go from there. This is my passion, my anger, the thing that fuels me in my work as a writing instructor and a WPA.

RECONCEIVING THE ROLE OF THE WPA

Since 1995 or so, I've worked in positions that were either explicitly called "writing program administrator" (or some derivative thereof, such as my current title, director of first-year writing) or included administrative responsibilities (such as a three-year stint directing a writing center). During that time, part of my challenge has been to take my personal perspectives, angers, and passions and ask: is it possible to include this in WPA work? Is it possible to separate it from that work? The question of WPA identity—what a WPA should do, should know, and what this work *is* is one that seems to periodically occupy the thoughts of many WPAs. In an essay providing advice for new WPAs, David Schwalm says that WPAs "cross the line" into administrative work, marking a space that is different from the one occupied by faculty (Schwalm 9). The definition (and status) of WPA work has its own mythology and its own central themes, many of which are connected with the quest for intellectual legitimacy. These include issues of mentoring and support for WPAs and recognition of WPA work as intellectual; the extent of the WPA's responsibility; renumeration for WPA work; the role of women in WPA positions; and the role that WPAs play in relation to university-level policies (e.g., L'Eplatteneir and Mastrangelo, "Why?"; Rose and Weiser 1999, 2002). In "The Politics of Writing Promotion," the analogy that Charles Schuster makes between WPAs and Boxer, the horse in *Animal Farm*, reflects the mythology surrounding these various issues. Just as Boxer works harder and longer than the other animals (and ultimately collapses doing so), Schuster says that WPAs

> are generally required to do more than their fair share of minding the farm. . . . The Puritans of English Departments, [WPAs] generally believe both in the ethos of work and, less fortunately, in the beneficence of authority. Their zeal to teach and serve smothers that other extremely useful instinct: self-survival through the salvation of publishing. Too often they lack the pragmatic, hard-edged, usually complicated, ironic intellectual footing of their colleagues who know that the system rewards a belief in self, not in community. Too often they believe that hard work, and hard work alone, will be their salvation. (Schuster 1991, 333)

Schuster's analogy resonates strongly with me (and, likely, with other WPAs) because it captures the elements of the mythology surrounding WPA work as we have developed and enacted it. We work hard; we believe in others sometimes at the expense of ourselves. The title of Diana George's collection, *Kitchen Cooks, Plate Twirlers and Troubadours*, also captures the conceptions that many WPAs have of ourselves as we juggle the many different aspects of the position: tending to our own tenure and promotion needs; working with others inside and outside of our writing programs to represent the interests of the program and students in it; and so on. In these conceptualizations, to some extent, we are both server (we develop things that help others; sometimes we "protect" others [students, instructors in our program] from incursions by others [other faculty, administrators, accrediting agencies, and so on]) and served (since we see ourselves, to a large extent legitimately, as existing at the mercy of a series of much larger [departmental, institutional, academic] cultures).

At the same time, this image of ourselves as WPAs also reflects elements of the progressive ideologies that are currently being used to frame discussions about education and educators. That is not surprising, of course—we exist within this system, so it is only logical that we should see ourselves and the work that we do inside of this frame. But in the same way that this frame precludes alternative stories about school (as Noddings suggests, the students are not assessed for their anxiety levels or dropout rates, but for levels of achievement on state-mandated exams), it also to some extent prescribes the roles that we define for ourselves as WPAs (and faculty members). In her essay in George's collection, Mara Holt chronicles the personal and professional tensions she experienced as she tried to bring her principles, such as a commitment to collaboration and transparency, into her own work. At the time the essay was written, Holt said that her

> struggle for voice remains. . . . I still get angry reactions from people for merely speaking my opinion. . . . The bottom line is this: The democratically-minded voices in my head most of the time outnumber the harsh voices of hierarchy-by-fiat trying to shut me up. . . . They have helped me fight for myself, to be on my own side. Further, when I am able to use my own power well, in the service of myself and others, I am energized. (Holt 1999, 39)

Holt's narrative introduces an element of feistiness not found in the mythology represented in Schuster's conceptualization of the WPA, a thread of passion and energy that may be the key for WPAs who want to change stories. Perhaps, then, this need to work strategically and from a point of principle raises a new component of the WPA identity not explicitly included in earlier conceptions like Schuster's, Holt's, or the others discussed here. Activist Rinku Sen reminds organizers that they are in many ways teachers; in the same way, we might begin to imagine what it would mean for our roles as WPAs and writing instructors if we began to think of ourselves as community organizers. I am deliberately using the word *organizer*, not *activist*, because *organizing* includes an explicit reference to deliberate, strategic planning and action that is sometimes not included in the notion of "activism." To return to the Karl Llewellyn quote, we *have* ideals, and ideals are at the core of activism. It's blending ideals and strategies that is the key to successful story-changing work.

As I've suggested here, the first step to story-changing work is not addressing the stories that we want to change, but building a base and developing alliances. Through interactions with community organizers, activists, and media strategists (and the literature that guides their work), I've come to understand that interest-, values-, and issue-based organizing provide three related approaches to this important initial work. While the primary focal points of these models differ, each shares a commitment to working from principle (even if the principle is that short-term victory is the most important goal, as in interest-based work), developing a broad base of support, cultivating leadership, and developing and acting on collaboratively developed messages. The process of developing these messages, too, must be strategic and systematic, regardless of the models that organizers—or WPAs—draw on for story-changing work.

Finally, I've suggested that story-changing work is most effectively enacted at the local level. It's easy to become concerned about actions that have the potential to substantially affect WPA work at the national level, such as the ED's moves to change assessment standards for accrediting bodies (discussed in chapter 1). But an individual WPA, or even a group of WPAs collaborating together, is but a fly on the windscreen of this approaching steamroller. On the other hand, working at the local level, we can develop assessment strategies within our own programs that reflect what *we* value, that ask questions and implement procedures that reflect what we know about best practices within our own courses and discipline. We can then use these assessments as bases for conversations beyond our programs—with our department chairs, our provosts, our university press officers, assessment coordinators, and presidents. Working bottom-up from our programs and top-down with our administrators, we can hope to provide alternative frames for these conversations that reflect our values and interests. We can also create events on our campuses, such as the Celebration of Student Writing at EMU, that provide alternative conceptions— and alternative frames—for discussions about writing and writers. These events, too, are important for the work of story-changing. And always, always, we can work from principle. As the questions embedded in chapters 4 and 5 demonstrate, the role of principle in story-changing work can vary, but it is always there. Our challenge is to blend ideals and strategies, so that we can shape the stories that are told about our programs, our work, and students every day.

APPENDIX
Contact Information for Community Organizations/ Media Strategists

Industrial Areas Foundation
www.industrialareasfoundation.org
National Office:
220 W. Kinzie Street, Fifth Floor
Chicago, IL 60610
312.245.9211
iaf@iafil.org

MoveOn.org
www.moveon.org

Moms Rising
www.momsrising.org

Real Reason
www.realreason.org
National Office:
55 Santa Clara Avenue, Suite 200
Oakland, CA 94610
510.444.5377
info@RealReason.org

Redefining Progress
www.rprogress.org
National Office:
1904 Franklin Street, Sixth Floor
Oakland, CA 94612
510.444.3041

Rockridge Institute
www.rockridgeinstitute.org
2105 Martin Luther King Jr. Way
Berkeley, CA 94704
(510) 204–0646

Norman Solomon
www.normansolomon.com

Strategic Press Information
Network (SPIN) Project
www.spinproject.org
National Office:
149 Natoma Street, Third Floor
San Francisco, CA 94105
415.227.4200

Wellstone Action
www.wellstoneaction.org
National Office:
821 Raymond Avenue, Suite 260
St. Paul, MN 55114
651.645.3939

NOTES

CHAPTER 1

1. All educational institutions, K-graduate, come under the auspices of an accrediting agency. Most colleges and universities fall under the auspices of one of the regional agencies: Middle States; North Central Association/Higher Learning Commission; New England Association of Schools and Colleges; Northwest Commission on Colleges and Universities; Southern Association of Colleges and Schools; or Western Association of Schools and Colleges. There are also hundreds of accrediting agencies for specialized educational institutions, from schools of acupuncture to barber colleges. Accreditation is often a requirement for federal funding; thus, if higher education institutions lose their accreditations, it is also likely that they will lose millions of dollars in federal (and state) funds that they receive.

CHAPTER 2

1. This approach to language instruction is borne out in some of Scott's addresses regarding writing (such as those collected in *The Standard of American Speech*), while some of the textbooks he wrote—often collaborating with coauthor Joseph Denney—seem more influenced by current-traditional rhetoric (e.g., *Elementary English Composition*).

CHAPTER 3

1. The strategy of providing overwhelming quantitative evidence to support assertions regarding education stemming from the Spellings Report has been used on occasions subsequent to the Report as well. In regional hearings on the report, Undersecretary of Higher Education Sarah Martinez Tucker opened each meeting with a rapid recitation of statistics about the number of students (including low income and minority students) who had "problems with student learning," though the sources of these statistics were never mentioned (Tucker, June 5 2005).
2. Despite a request to ACT for the questionnaire distributed to survey respondents (e-mail correspondence, April 30, 2007), I have been unable to access a copy of the actual survey, thus the description of the survey represents a best guess regarding survey construction extracted from the reporting of results included in the NCS *Report*.
3. Respondents were asked to use a Likert scale ranking from 1 (not important) to 5 (very important) to indicate the degree of emphasis

they placed on instruction in the given area: "Composition Process and Purpose" (24 items); "Topic and Idea Development" (14 items); "Organization, Unity, and Coherence" (8 items); "Word Choice in Terms of Style, Tone, Clarity, and Economy" (8 items); "Sentence Structure and Formation" (7 items); "Conventions of Usage" (7 items); "Conventions of Punctuation" (11 items); and "Evaluation of Writing" (10 items) (39–40). (Presumably, these questions map onto the "Test Specifications for the EPAS English/Writing" exam described later in the report, which include questions about "punctuation"; "grammar and usage"; "sentence structure"; "strategy"; "organization"; and "style" (54–55). (All categories except "Evaluation of Writing" included a choice of "other" and asked for respondents to specify; although the *Report* includes the mean rating for these "other" choices and indicates the standard deviation for this line, there is no indication of the responses that were submitted or specifics provided by respondents.)

4.   ACT's 2005 revenue (the latest available via Guidestar, a database of nonprofit organizations) was $179,333,056. Of that, ACT spent $131,681,560 on "the administration of research, testing, measurement, and evaluative programs in all types and kinds of educational endeavors; and the advancement of the interpretation and dissemination of information resulting from such programs" (ACT Form 990). ACT also spent $110,930 on "attempt[ing] to influence national, state, or local legislation, including any attempt to influence public opinion on a legislative matter or referendum" (ACT Form 990). All proceeds generated by ACT's various products are put back into the company in the form of salaries, research (such as the NCS), dissemination (such as reports), and so on. The NCS is but one of the research tools included in the more than $131 million spent by ACT on "research, testing, measurement, and evaluative programs" (ACT IRS Form 990).

5.   The SAT unveiled in early 2005 included the new writing exam, created in part in response to pressure from the University of California beginning in 2001. George Gadda, assistant director of the UCLA Writing Programs, was enlisted to chair the group developing the exam (SAT site). The revised exam, to be completed in an hour, consists of a multiple-choice test of grammatical conventions (to be completed in 35 minutes) and a timed writing experience (to be completed in 25). In the writing portion of the exam, students are to "develop a point of view on an issue presented in an excerpt; support your point of view using reasoning and examples from your reading, studies, experiences, or observations; and follow the conventions of standard written English" in an essay (SAT).

CHAPTER 4

1.   As with the other school-based vignettes in this chapter and the next, this is a pseudonym.

2.   There is some dispute—among activists, and among linguists and other academics—as to the specific role of language in this change; one criticism of the work of Rockridge and Lakoff is that their work can be seen

as suggesting that developing new frames can *create* change. Before Democrats (or anyone else) develop these frames, though, critics argue they need to come up with some new *content*, in the form of ideas and narratives, to put a frame around (see, e.g., Nunberg 2006).

CHAPTER 6

1. Most Jews believe that there is not one way to be Jewish (though some, like Hasidic or ultraorthodox Jews, might adamantly disagree). The different approaches to Judaic culture and practice are reflected in the various strands of Judaism. Hasidism, orthodox (though there are significant differences between ultra and modern), conservative, reform, reconstructionist, and secular humanism are *all* approaches to Jewish observation that fall under the "big tent" of Judaic culture and practice. While each group shares common roots in Judaic culture and a common allegiance to principles of that culture (that is, a common cultural identity *as* Jews), the differences between a Hasidic Jew and a secular humanist are substantial and span epistemologies, ideas, ideologies, lifestyles, and practices.

REFERENCES

ACT. 2007a. *National Curriculum Survey, 2005–2006.* Iowa City: ACT.

ACT. 2007b. New study ponts to gap between U.S. high school curriculum and college expectations. http://www.act.org/news/releases/2007/04–09–07.html.

Achieve.org. 2007. Home page.f http://www.achieve.org.

Adams, Peter Dow. 1993. Basic writing reconsidered. *Journal of Basic Writing* 21 (1): 22–35.

Addams, Jane. 1911. Twenty years at Hull House. New York: Macmillan.

Adler-Kassner, Linda. 2005. Framing the SAT writing exam. Modern Language Association Conference, Washington, D.C.

———, and Heidi Estrem. 2003. Rethinking researched writing: Public literacy in the composition classroom. *WPA Journal* 26 (3): 119–31.

———, and Susanmarie Harrington, ed. 2001. *Questioning authority: Stories told in school.* Ann Arbor: University of Michigan Press.

———, Chris Anson, and Rebecca Howard. Forthcoming. Framing plagiarism. In *Originality, imitation, and plagiarism,* ed. Martha Vicinus and Caroline Eisner. Ann Arbor: University of Michigan Press.

Akin, Rebecca. 2005. Foreword. In *Teaching as principled practice,* ed. Linda Kroll et al., xvii–xxii. Thousand Oaks, CA: Sage.

Alex, Patricia. 2007. SAT optional at many New Jersey colleges. *Record.* November 19, 1.

Alinsky, Saul.1946. *Reveille for radicals.* New York: Vintage, 1989.

———. 1971. *Rules for radicals.* New York: Vintage.

Allington, Richard, ed. 2002. *Big Brother and the National Reading Curriculum: How ideology trumped evidence.* Portsmouth, NH: Heinemann.

Altwerger, Bess. 2005a. Reading for profit: A corporate coup in context. In *Reading for profit: How the bottom line leaves kids behind,* ed. Bess Altwerger, 1–20. Portsmouth, NH: Heinemann.

———. 2005b. *Reading for profit: How the bottom line leaves kids behind.* Portsmouth, NH: Heinemann.

American Association of Colleges and Universities. *AAC&U statement on Spellings Commission draft report.* http://www.aacu.org/About/statements/SpellingsFinalDraft.cfm (accessed August 8, 2006).

American opportunity: A communications toolkit. 2006. San Francisco/New York: Opportunity Agenda/SPIN Project.

Bagdikian, Ben. 1995. *The media monopoly.* 5th ed., Boston: Beacon Press.

Ball, Arnetha, Linda Christensen, Cathy Fleischer, Richard Haswell, Jean Ketter, Robert Yagelski, and Kathleen Blake Yancey. 2005. *The impact of the SAT and ACT timed writing tests.* Urbana, IL: NCTE.

Bartholomae, David. 1985. Inventing the university. In *When a writer can't write: Studies in writer's block and other composing process problems,* ed. Mike Rose, 134–65. New York: Guilford.

———. 2005. Living in style. In *Writing on the margins*, ed. David Bartholomae, 1–16. Boston: Bedford St. Martin's.

Bawarshi, Anis. 2003. *Genre and the invention of the writer*. Logan: Utah State University Press.

Berlin, James. 1987. *Rhetoric and reality: Writing instruction in American colleges*. Carbondale: Southern Illinois University Press.

Bercovitch, Sacvan. 1978. *The American jeremiad*. Madison: University of Wisconsin Press.

Berdik, Chris. 2005. Teachers fight high-tech cheaters. *Boston Globe*, February 27, 10.

Blades, Joan. 2006. Interview by Linda Adler-Kassner. September 12, 2006. Berkeley, CA.

Bloom, Lynn. 1995. Making a difference: Writing program administration as a creative process. In *Resituating writing: Constructing and administering writing programs*, ed. Joseph Janangelo and Kristine Hansen, 73–81.

Bodmer, Paul. 2007. Interview. July 8, 2007. Tempe, AZ.

Bogart, Glenn. 2007. Comment on Explaining the accreditation debate. *Inside higher education*. (see Lederman, 2007b).

Bosquet, Marc. 2004. Composition as management science. In *Tenured bosses and disposable teachers: Writing instruction in the managed university*, ed. Marc Bosquet, Tony Scott, and Leo Parascondola, 11–34. Carbondale, IL: Southern Illinois University Press.

Bosquet, Marc, Tony Scott, and Leo Parascondola, ed. 2004. *Tenured bosses and disposable teachers: Writing instruction in the managed university*. Carbondale, IL: Southern Illinois University Press.

Bowden, Darsie. 2007. Walk it out: The *chi* of writing program administration. Paper presented at the annual meeting of the Council of Writing Program Administrators. Tempe, AZ.

Brandt, Deborah. 1998. Sponsors of literacy. *College Composition and Communication* 49 (2): 165–85.

Brandt, Deborah. 2001. Protecting the personal. In Symposium: the politics of the personal; Storying our lives against the grain. *College English* 64 (1): 42–44.

Bray, Robert. 2000. *Spin works!* San Francisco: SPIN Project.

Breger, Marshall J., ed. 2003. *Public policy and social issues: Jewish sources and perspectives*. Westport, CT: Praeger.

Broad, Bob. 2003. *What we really value: Beyond rubrics in teaching and assessing writing*. Logan: Utah State University Press.

Brown, John Seely. 2005. Narrative as a knowledge medium in organizations. In *Storytelling in organizations: Why storytelling is transforming 21st century organizations and management*, ed. John Seely Brown, Stephen Denning, Katalina Goh, and Laurence Prusak, 53–95. Oxford: Elesevier Butterworth-Heinemann.

Brown, John Seely, Stephen Denning, Katalina Groh, and Laurence Prusak, ed. 2005. *Storytelling in organizations: Why storytelling is transforming 21st century organizations and management*. Oxford: Elesevier Butterworth-Heinemann.

Brown, J. Stanley. 1905. The ideal secondary school teacher. *The Fourth Yearbook of the National Society of the Scientific Study of Education* :29–32.

Budner, Bruce. 2006. Interview by Linda Adler-Kassner. September 14, 2006. Berkeley, CA.

Cambridge, Barbara, and Ben McClelland.1995. From icon to partner: Repositioning the Writing Program Administrator. In *Resituating writing*, ed. Joseph Janangelo and Kristine Hansen, 151–59. Portsmouth, NH: Boynton/Cook.

Carey, James. 1989. *Communication as culture: Essays on media and society.* Winchester, MA: Unwin Hyman.

——. 1997a. The press, public opinion, and public discourse. In *James Carey: A critical reader*, ed. Eve Stryker Munson and Catherine A. Warren, 228–57. Minneapolis: University of Minnesota Press.

———. 1997b. A republic, if you can keep it: Liberty and public life in the age of glasnost. In *James Carey: A critical reader*, ed. Eve Stryker Munson and Catherine A. Warren, 207–27. Minneapolis: University of Minnesota Press.

Cerulo, Karen, ed. 2002. *Culture in mind: Toward a sociology of culture and cognition.* New York: Routledge.

Chambers, John Whiteclay. 1992. *The tyranny of change: America in the progressive era 1890–1920.* New York: St. Martin's Press.

Chambers, Edward, and Michael Cowan. 2003. *Roots for radicals: Organizing for power, action, and justice.* New York: Continuum.

Chiseri-Strater, Elizabeth. 1991. *Academic literacies: The public and private discourse of university students.* Portsmouth, NH: Heinemann.

Chute, Eleanor. 2007. Colleges still unsure how to use new SAT. *Pittsburgh Post Gazette*, February 25, A1.

Coles, Robert. 1989. *The call of stories.* New York: Houghton Mifflin.

Cortes, Ernesto. 2006. Toward a democratic culture. *The Kettering Review* 24 (1): 46–57.

Cremin, Lawrence. 1988. *American education: The metropolitan experience, 1876–1980.* New York: Harper and Row.

Cushman, Ellen. 1999. The public intellectual, service learning, and activist research. *College English* 61 (3): 328–36.

———. 2001. The butterfly fix(at)ion. In Symposium: The politics of the personal; Storying our lives against the grain. *College English* 64 (1): 44–46.

———. 2002. Sustainable service-learning programs. *College Composition and Communication* 54 (1): 40–65.

Czitrom, Daniel. 1983. *Media and the American mind: From Morse to Mcluhan.* Chapel Hill: University of North Carolina Press.

Davis, Millie. 2005. *Going public: Back story on the success of the SAT/ACT task force report.* Unpublished memo. Urbana, IL: National Council of Teachers of English.

Deacon, David, Michael Pickering, Peter Golding, and Graham Murdock. 1999. *Researching communications.* London: Arnold.

Deans, Tom. 2000. *Writing partnerships: Service-learning in composition.* Urbana, IL: NCTE.

deCerteau, Michel. 1984. *The practice of everyday life.* Minneapolis: University of Minnesota Press.

Desmet, Christy. 2005. Beyond accommodation: Individual and collective in a large writing program. In *Discord and direction: The postmodern Writing Program*

Administrator, ed. Sharon James McGee and Carolyn Handa, 40–58. Logan: Utah State University Press.

DeVise, Daniel. 2006. Grammar is making a comeback; poor writing skills among teens and a new section of SAT fuel return to language basics. *Houston Chronicle,* October 29, A2.

Dewey, John. 1916. *Democracy and education.* New York: Free Press.

Dobbs, Michael. 2005. Teachers give new SAT essay low marks. *Washington Post,* May 4, 10.

Dorff, Elliot N., and Louis E. Newman, ed. 1995. *Contemporary Jewish ethics and morality.* New York: Oxford University Press.

Douglas, Susan. 1994. *Where the girls are: Growing up female with the mass media.* New York: Times Books.

Dudley-Marling, Curt. 1997. *Living with uncertainty: The messy reality of classroom practice.* Portsmouth, NH: Heinemann.

Elazar, Daniel J. 1997. *Kinship and consent: The Jewish political tradition and its contemporary uses.* 2nd ed., New Brunswick, NJ: Transaction Publishers.

Elbow, Peter. 2000a. *Everyone can write.* New York: Oxford University Press.

———. 2000b. Getting along without grades—and getting along with them, too. In *Everyone can write,* ed. Peter Elbow, 399–421. New York: Oxford University Press.

———. 2000c. High stakes and low stakes in responding to student writing. In *Everyone can write,* ed. Peter Elbow, 351–59. New York: Oxford University Press.

———. 2000d. Premises and foundations. In *Everyone can write,* ed. Peter Elbow, 1–3. New York: Oxford University Press.

Emery, Kathy, and Susan Ohanian. 2004. *Why is corporate America bashing our public schools?* Portsmouth, NH: Heinemann.

Engel, Lawrence J. 2002. Saul D. Alinsky and the Chicago School. *Journal of Speculative Philosophy* 16 (1): 50–66.

NCTE Executive Committee. 2004. NCTE beliefs about the teaching of writing. http://www.ncte.org/prog/writing/research/118876.htm (accessed November 11, 2006).

Fairclough, Norman. 1992. *Discourse and social change.* Cambridge: Polity.

FairTest.org. Home page.

Feldmeier, Julia. 2005. Anxious students brace for new SAT. *Washington Post,* March 10, T3.

Ferguson, Richard. 2006. A message from ACT's CEO. In *Breaking barriers: Ensuring college and career success.* ACT.

Fleischer, Cathy. 2000. *Teachers organizing for change: Making literacy learning everybody's business.* Urbana, IL: NCTE.

Fleischer, Cathy, and David Schaafsma, ed. 1998. *Literacy and democracy: Teacher research and composition studies in pursuit of habitable spaces.* Urbana, IL: NCTE.

Foster, Andrea. 2006. Students fall short on information literacy, Educational Testing Service's study finds. *The Chronicle of Higher Education,* October 27.

Fox, Tom. 1999. *Defending access: A critique of standards in higher education.* Portsmouth, NH: Boynton.

Foxworthy, Natalie. 2005. Online plagiarism on rise. *News Record,* January 13.

Franek, Mark. 2005. New SAT writing section scores low. *Christian Science Monitor.*

Freire, Paulo. 1998. *Pedagogy of freedom: Ethics, democracy, and civic courage.* Lanham, MD: Rowan and Littlefield.

Gamson, William A. 1991. Commitment and agency in social movements. *Sociological Forum* 6 (1): 27–50.

———, David Croteau, William Hoynes, and Theodore Sasson. 1992. Media images and the social construction of reality. *Annual Review of Sociology* 18: 373–93.

Garan, Elaine M. 2005. Scientific flimflam: A who's who of entrepreneurial research. In *Reading for profit: How the bottom line leaves kids behind,* ed. Bess Altwerger, 21–32. Portsmouth, NH: Heinemann.

Gaylin, Willard, Ira Glasser, Steven Marcus, and David Rothman, ed. 1978. *Doing good: The limits of benevolence.* New York: Pantheon.

Gee, James. 1996. *Social linguistics and literacies.* 2nd ed., London: Taylor and Francis.

Gelobter, Michel. 2006. Interview by Linda Adler-Kassner. September 13, 2006. Oakland, CA.

Gelobter, Michael et al. 2005. Standing on whose shoulders? Why race and class matter to the environmental movement. http://www.grist.org/comments/soapbox/2005/05/27/gelobter-soul/ (accessed February 12).

George, Diana. 1999. Introduction. In *Kitchen cooks, plate twirlers and troubadours: Writing Program Administrators tell their stories,* ed. Diana George, xi–xiv. Portsmouth, NH: Boynton/Cook.

Gere, Ann Ruggles. 2001. Articles of faith. In Symposium: The politics of the personal; Storying our lives against the grain. *College English* 64 (1): 46–47.

Gilroy, Marilyn. 2004. Cut and paste cheating: Rampant, but amenable to faculty action. *Ethnic News,* December 13, 30–32.

Giroux, Henry. 1980. Beyond the correspondence theory: Notes on the dynamics of reproduction and transformation. *Curriculum Inquiry* 10 (3): 225–47.

Glod, Maria and Jay Matthews. 2006. Some allowed to sit out the SAT; admission requirement will be waived for select students. *Washington Post.* May 25.

Goldblatt, Eli. 2005. Alinsky's reveille: A community-organizing model for neighborhood-based literacy projects. *College English* 67 (3): 274–95.

Goldenberg, Robert. 1984. Talmud. In *Back to the sources,* ed Barry W. Holtz, 129–176. New York: Simon and Schuster.

Graff, Harvey. 1979. *The literacy myth.* New York: Academic Press.

Grego, Rhonda, and Nancy Thompson. 1996. Repositioning remediation: Renegotiating composition's work in the academy. *College Composition and Communication* 47 (1): 62–84.

Gunner, Jeanne. 1998. Iconic discourse: The troubling legacy of Mina Shaughnessy. *Journal of Basic Writing* 19 (2): 25–42.

Gustafson, Roger, ed. 2000. *Power, justice, faith: Conversations with the I.A.F.* Center for Religion and Civic Culture, University of Southern California.

Hall, Stuart. 1984. The narrative construction of reality. *Southern Review* 17: 1–17.

Hammer, Melanie. 2005. Creative writing it isn't. *Newsday,* March 20, 40.

Hanh, Thich Nhat. 1992. *Peace is in every step.* New York: Bantam Books.

Hansen, Kristine. 1995. Face to face with part-timers: Ethics and the professionalization of writing faculties. . In *Resituating writing: Constructing and administering writing programs*, ed. Joseph Janangelo and Kristine Hansen, 23–45. Portsmouth, NH: Boynton-Cook.

Hanson, Russell. 1985. *The democratic imagination in America: Conversations with our past*. Princeton, NJ: Princeton University Press.

Harrington, Susanmarie, and Linda Adler-Kassner. 1998. The dilemma that still counts: Basic writing at a political crossroads. *Journal of Basic Writing* 17 (2): 1–24.

Harris, Joseph. 1997. *A teaching subject: Composition since 1966*. Upper Saddle River, NJ: Prentice Hall.

———. 2000. Meet the new boss, same as the old boss: Class consciousness in composition. *College Composition and Communication* 52 (1): 43–68.

Hartzog, Carol. 1986. *Composition and the academy: A study of Writing Program Administration*. New York: MLA.

Haswell, Richard. 1988. Dark shadows: The fate of writers at the bottom. *College Composition and Communication* 39 (3): 303–14.

———. 2005. NCTE/CCCC's recent war on scholarship. *Written Communication* 22 (2): 198–223.

Heath, Shirley Brice. 1983. *Ways with words*. Cambridge: Cambridge University Press.

Helmers, Marguerite. 1994. *Writing students: Composition testimonials and representations of students*. Albany: State University of New York Press.

Hertog, James K., and Douglas M. McLeod. 2001. A multiperspectival approach to framing analysis: A field guide. In *Framing public life*, ed. Stephen D. Reese, Oscar H. Gandy, and August E. Grant, 139–61. Mahwah, NJ: Lawrence Erlbaum.

Herzberg, Bruce. 1994. Community service and critical teaching. *College Composition and Communication* 45 (3): 307–19.

———. 1995. Response. *College Composition and Communication* 46 (4): 555–56.

Hesse, Douglas. 1999. The WPA as father, husband, ex. In *Kitchen cooks, plate twirlers, and troubadours*, ed. Diana George, 44–55. Portsmouth, NH: Boyton/Cook.

———. 2001. Stories, style, and the exploitation of experience. In *Questioning authority: Stories told in school*, ed. Linda Adler-Kassner and Susanmarie Harrington, 19–33. Ann Arbor: University of Michigan Press.

Hofstadter, Richard. 1955. *The age of reform: From Bryant to F.D.R.* New York: Alfred A. Knopf.

Holmes, Erin. 2005. Freaking out about the new SAT? Some teens are. *Chicago Daily Herald*, August 8, 1.

Holt, Mara. 1999. On coming to voice. In *Kitchen cooks, plate twirlers, and troubadours*, ed. Diana George, 26–43. Portsmouth, NH: Boyton/Cook.

hooks, bell. 1994. *Teaching to transgress: Education as the practice of freedom*. New York: Routledge.

Howard, Rebecca Moore. 2004. Plagiarism epidemics, media epidemics. *Colby College*, March 4.

Hull, Glynda, and Mike Rose. 1990. This wooden shack place: The logic of an unconventional reading. *College Composition and Communication* 41 (3): 287–98.

196   THE ACTIVIST WPA

Huot, Brian. 2002. *(Re)Articulating writing assessment for teaching and learning.* Logan: Utah State University Press.

Israel, Richard J.1995. Jewish tradition and political action. In *Contemporary Jewish ethics and morality,* ed. Elliot N. Dorff and Louis E. Newman, 118–28. New York: Oxford University Press.

Iyengar, Shanto. 1991. *Is anyone responsible? How television frames political issues.* Chicago: University of Chicago Press.

Jacobs, Dale, and Laura Micciche, ed. 2003. *A way to move: Rhetorics of emotion and composition studies.* Portsmouth, NH: Boynton/Cook.

James, William. 1910a. *Pragmatism: A new name for some old ways of thinking.* New York: Longmans, Green and Company.

———. 1910b. What pragmatism means. In *Pragmatism: A new name for some old ways of thinking,* 43–80. New York: Longman, Greens and Company.

Janangelo, Joseph. 1995. Theorizing difference and negotiating differends: (Un)naming writing programs' many complexitities and strengths. In *Resituating writing: Constructing and administering writing programs,* ed. Joseph Janangelo and Kristine Hansen, 3–22.

Janangelo, Joseph, and Kristine Hansen, ed.1995. *Resituating writing: Constructing and administering writing programs.* Portsmouth, NH: Boynton/Cook.

Jenkins, Alan. 2006. Paper presented to the Tides Institute. San Francisco, CA.

Kellner, Menachem Mark. 1995. The structure of Jewish ethics. In *Contemporary Jewish ethics and morality,* ed. Elliot N. Dorff and Louis E. Newman, 12–24. New York: Oxford University Press.

Klein, Karen. 2005. How I gamed the SAT. *Los Angeles Times,* April 3.

Kliksberg, Bernardo. 2003. *Social justice: A Jewish perspective.* Jerusalem: Gefen Publishing/World Jewish Congress.

Kohl, Herbert. 1968. *36 children.* New York: New American Library.

Kohn, Alfie. 2000. *The case against standardized testing: Raising the scores, ruining the schools.* Portsmouth, NH: Heinemann.

Kollali, Sapna. 2005. First SAT exams with essays unveiled Saturday. *Post-Standard,* March 10, 1.

Kolodny, Annette. 1975. *The lay of the land: Metaphor as experience and history in American life and letters.* Chapel Hill: University of North Carolina Press.

Kroll, Linda, Ruth Cossey, David Donahue, Tomas Galguera, Vicki Kubler LaBoskey, Anna Ershler Richert, and Philip Tucher. 2005. *Teaching as principled practice: Managing complexity for social justice.* Thousand Oaks, CA: Sage.

Krone, Emily. 2006. Colleges: Students are not prepared, more freshman need remedial help, statistics show. *Chicago Daily Herald,* December 3, 1.

Kula, Irwin. 2006. *Yearnings: Embracing the sacred messiness of life.* New York: Hyperion.

Lakoff, George. 2002. *Moral politics: How liberals and conservatives think.* 2nd ed., Chicago: University of Chicago Press.

———. 2004. *Don't think of an elephant! Know your values and frame the debate.* White River Junction, VT: Chelsea Green.

———. 2006. *Thinking points: Communicating our American values and visions.* New York: Farrar, Straus and Giroux.

Lalicker, William. 2007. E-mail to Conference on Basic Writing Listserv. March 13, 2007.

Lederman, Doug. 2007a. Another front on accreditation. *Inside Higher Education*, http://www.insidehighered.com/layout/set/print/news/2007/01/07/accredit (accessed January 1, 2007).

———. 2007b. Explaining the accreditation debate. *Inside Higher Education*, http://www.insiderhighered.com/layout/set/print/news/2007/03/29/accredit (accessed March 29, 2007).

———. 2007c. Fault lines on accreditation. *Inside Higher Education*, http://www.insidehighered.com/layout/set/print/news/2007/02/22/accredit (accessed February 22, 2007).

———. 2007d. Huge ipeds lives. *Inside Higher Education*, http://www.insidehighered.com/layout/set/print/news/2007/02/19/ipeds (accessed February 19, 2007).

———. 2007e. Lack of consenus on lack of consensus. *Inside Higher Education*, http://insidehighered.com/news/2007/06/04/accredit (accessed January 12, 2007).

———. 2007f. The new top fed for higher ed. *Inside Higher Education*, http://www.insidehighered.com/news/2007/01/03/tucker (accessed January 3, 2007).

———. 2007g. U.S. accreditation official out of a job. *Inside Higher Education*, http://www.insidehighered.com/layout/set/print/news/2007/1/29/barth (accessed January 29, 2007).

———.2007h. When is student learning 'good enough'? *Inside Higher Education*, http://www.insidehighered.com/layout/set/print/news/2007/02/23/accredit (accessed February 23, 2007).

L'Eplatteneir, Barbara and Lisa Mastrangelo. 2004. Why administrative histories? In *Historical studies of writing program administration: individuals, communities, and the formation of a discipline*. Ed. Barbara L'Eplatteneir and Lisa Mastrangelo, xvii-xxvii. West Lafayette, IN: Parlor Press.

Lippmann, Walter. 1922. *Public opinion*. New York: Harcourt, Brace, and Company.

Lynne, Patricia. 2004. *Coming to terms: A theory of writing assessment*. Logan: Utah State University Press.

Marciszewski, April. 2005. Colleges take byte out of cheating. *Tulsa Herald*, 9.

Marciszewski, April. 2005. Colleges take byte out of cheating. *Tulsa World*, February 1, 9.

Markelein, Mary Beth. 2007. Schoolteachers, professors differ on what students should know. *USA Today*, April 9.

Mastrangelo, L'Eplattenier Barbara and Lisa. 2004. Why administrative histories? In *Historical Studies of Writing Program Administration*, xvii–xxvi. West Lafayette, IN: Parlor Press.

Mathieu, Paula. 2005. *Tactics of hope: The public turn in English composition*. Portsmouth, NH: Boynton/Cook-Heinemann.

May, Elaine Tyler. 1988. *Homeward bound: American families in the Cold War era*. New York: Basic Books.

McChesney, Robert. 2005. Russell Newman, and Ben Waters, ed. *The future of media: Resistance and reform in the 21st century*. New York: Seven Stories Press.

McDonald, John. 2005. Council of Writing Program Administrators Network for Media Action workshop at annual convention of CCCC.

McGrath, Charles. 2004. Writing to the test. *New York Times*, November 7, 24.

McKnight, Douglas. 2003. *Schooling, the Puritan imperative, and the molding of an American national identity*. Mahwah, NJ: Lawrence Erlbaum.

McLeod, Susan.1995. The foreigner: WAC directors as agents of change. In *Resituating Writing*, ed. Joseph Janangelo and Kristine Hansen, 108–116. Portsmouth, NH: Boynton/Cook.

Micciche, Laura. 2002. More than a feeling: Disappointment and WPA work. *College English* 64 (4): 432–58.

Miller, Charles et al. 2006. *A test of leadership: Charting the future of U.S. higher education*. Washington D.C.: Department of Education.

Miller, Keith D., and Jennifer M. Santos. 2005. Recomposing religious plotlines. In *Negotiating religious faith in the composition classroom*, ed. Elizabeth Vander Lei and Bonnie Lenore Kyburz, 63–83. Portsmouth, NH: Boynton/Cook-Heinemann.

Miller, Richard. 1998. *As if learning mattered: Reforming higher education*. Ithaca, NY: Cornell University Press.

———, and Michael J. Cripps. 2005. Minimum qualifications: Who should teach first year writing? In *Discord and direction: The postmodern Writing Program Administrator*, ed. Sharon James McGee and Carolyn Handa, 123–39. Logan: Utah State University Press.

Milroy, Eleanor. 2006. Interview by Linda Adler-Kassner.

Moore, Michael. 2004. *Fahrenheit 911*. Dir. Michael Moore.

Mortensen, Peter. 1998. Going public. *College Composition and Communication* 50 (2): 182–205.

MoveOn.org. 2004. *Moveon's 50 ways to love your country*. Maui, HI: Inner Ocean.

Munson, Eve Stryker, and Catherine A. Warren, ed. 1997. *James Carey: A critical reader*. Minneapolis: University of Minnesota Press.

Mutnick, Deborah. 1996. *Writing in an alien world: Basic writing and the struggle for equality in higher education*. Portsmouth, NH: Boynton.

NCTE. 2004. NCTE beliefs about the teaching of writing. http://www.ncte.org/about/over/positions/category/write/118876.htm?source=gs (accessed July 2, 2006).

NCTE. 2006. NCTE praises Reading First audit, calls for further investigation. http://www.ncte.org/about/press/key/125668.htm?source=gs (accessed October 10, 2006).

NCTE Assessment and Testing Study Group. 2004. Framing statements on assessment. http://www.ncte.org/about/over/positions/category/assess/118875.htm (accessed February 7, 2007).

No Child Left Behind executive summary. 2001. U.S. Department of Education. Washington, DC: U.S Government. http://www.ed.gov/nclb/overview/intro/execsumm.html. (accessed January 13, 2006)

Noble, David W. 1985. *The end of American history*. Minneapolis: University of Minnesota Press.

Noddings, Nell. 2005. *The challenge to care in schools: An alternative approach to education*. New York: Teachers College Press.

Nunberg, Geoffrey. 2006. *Talking right*. New York: Public Affairs.

Ohanian, Susan. 2001. *Caught in the middle: Nonstandard kids and a killing curriculum*. Portsmouth: Heinemann.

O'Neill, Peggy, Ellen Schendel, and Brian Huot. 2002. Defining assessment as research. *WPA Journal* 26 (1/2): 10–26.

Opportunity Agenda. 2006. *The state of opportunity in America: Executive summary.* New York: Opportunity Agenda.

O'Reilley, Mary Rose. 2005a. *The garden at night: Burnout and breakdown in the teaching life.* Portsmouth, NH: Heinemann.

———. 2005b. *The peaceable classroom.* Portsmouth, NH: Boynton/Cook-Heinemann.

Oakes, Jennie, and Martin Lipton. 2003. *Teaching to change the world.* 2nd ed., Boston: McGraw Hill.

Oaman, Howard A., and Samuel M. Craver. 1995. *Philosophical foundations of education.* Upper Saddle River, NJ: Prentice-Hall.

O'Neill, Peggy. 2003. Moving beyond holistic scoring through validity inquiry. *Journal of Writing Assessment* 1 (1): 47–65.

Ornstein, Allen, and Daniel Levine. 2003. *Foundations of education.* 8th ed., Boston: Houghton Mifflin.

Ozmon, Howard, and Samuel Craver. 1995. *Philosophical foundations of education.* Upper Saddle River, NJ: Prentice Hall.

Palmer, Parker. 1998. *The courage to teach: Exploring the inner landscapes of a teacher's life.* San Francisco: Jossey-Bass.

Peck, Wayne Cambell, Lorraine Higgins, and Linda Flower.1995. Community literacy. *College Composition and Communication* 46 (2): 199–222.

Perelman, Leslie. 2005. New SAT: Write long, badly, and prosper. *Los Angeles Times,* May 29, 5.

Peterson, Erik. 2006. Interview by Linda Adler-Kassner. rural Illinois, October 4, 2006.

———. 2007. Interview by Linda Adler-Kassner. Telephone, February 12, 2007.

Prusak, Laurence. 2005. Storytelling in organizations. In *Storytelling in organizations,* ed. John Seeley Brown, Stephen Denning, Katalina Groh, and Laurence Prusak, 15–51. Oxford: Elesevier Butterworth-Heinemann.

Pulliam, John D., and James J. Van Patten. 2007. *History of education in America.* 9th ed. Upper Saddle River, NJ: Prentice-Hall.

Putnam, Robert, and Lewis M. Feldstein. *Better together: Restoring the American community.* New York: Simon and Schuster.

Rea, Louis M., and Richard A. Parker.1992. *Designing and conducting survey research: A comprehensive guide.* San Francisco: Jossey-Bass.

Ready or not: Creating a high school diploma that counts. American Diploma Project, 2004.

Reese, Stephen D. 2001. Prologue-Framing public life: A bridging model for media research. In Framing public life perspecitves on media and our understanding of the social world ed. Stephen D. Reese, Oscar H. Gandy, and August E. Grant, 7–31. Mahwah, NJ: Lawrence Erlbaum.

Reese, Stephen D., Oscar H. Gandy, and August E. Grant, ed. 2001. *Framing public life: Perspectives on media and our understanding of the social world.* LEA's Communication Series, ed. Jennings Bryant and Dolf Zillman. Mahwah, NJ: Lawrence Erlbaum.

Robinson, Jay. 1998. Literacy and lived lives: Reflections on the responsibilities of teachers. In *Literacy and democracy*, ed. Cathy Fleischer and David Schaafsma, 1–27. Urbana, IL: NCTE.

Roebuck, Karin. 2005. New SAT introduces fear factor. *Tribune Review*, March 10.

Rogers, Mary Beth. 1990. *Cold anger: A story of faith and power politics*. Denton: University of North Texas Press.

Romano, Susan, and Lester Faigley. 1995. Going electronic: Creating multiple sites for innovation in a writing program. In *Resituating writing*, ed. Joseph Janangelo and Kristine Hansen, 146–58. Portsmouth, NH: Boynton/Cook.

Rose, Mike. 1985. The language of exclusion: Writing instruction at the university. *College English* 47 (4): 341–59.

———. 2006a. *An open language: Selected writing on literacy, learning, and opportunity*. Boston: Bedford-St. Martin's.

———. 2006b. Introduction (to part six). In *An open language*, ed. Mike Rose, 407–410. Boston: Bedford-St. Martin's.

Rose, Shirley K., and Irwin Weiser, ed. 1999. *The Writing Program Administrator as researcher: Inquiry in action and reflection*. Portsmouth, NH: Heinemann-Boynton/Cook..

———. 2002. *The Writing Program Administrator as theorist: Making knowledge work*. Portsmouth, NH: Heinemann-Boynton/Cook.

Roskelley, Hepzibah, and Ronald Kate. 1998. *Reason to believe: Romanticism, pragmatism, and the teaching of writing*. Albany: State University of New York Press.

Rothman, David J. 1978. The state as parent: Social policy in the Progressive Era. In *Doing good: The limits of benevolence*, ed. Willard Gaylin, Ira Glasser, Steven Marcus, and David Rothman, 67–95. New York: Pantheon.

Royer, Daniel, and Roger Gilles. 1998. Directed Self-Placement: An attitude of orientation. *College Composition and Communication* 50 (1): 54–70.

Royster, Jacqueline. 2002. Academic discourses, or small boats on big seas. In *Alt Dis: Alternative Discourses and the Academy*, ed. Christopher Schroeder, Helen Fox, and Patricia Bizzell, 23–30. Portsmouth, NH: Boynton/Cook.

Russo, John, and Andrew Banks. 1996. Teaching the organizing model of unionism and campaign-based education: National and international trends. In *AFL-CIO/Cornell University Research Conference on union organizing*. Washington D.C.

Ryan, Charlotte. 1991. *Prime time activism: Media strategies for grassroots organizing*. Boston: South End Press.

Ryan, Charlotte, Kevin Caragee, and William Meinhofer. 2001. Framing, the news media, and collective action. *Journal of Broadcasting and Electronic Media* 45 (1): 175–82.

Sacks, Jonathan. 2003. Tikkun Olam: Perfecting God's word. In *Public policy and social issues: Jewish sources and perspectives*, ed. Marshall J. Breger, 35–48. Westport, CT: Praeger.

Schatz, David, Chaim I. Wasman, and Nathan J. Diament, ed. 1997. *Tikkun Olam: Social responsibility in Jewish law and thought*. Northvale, NJ: Jason Aronson.

Schell, Eileen E. 1998. *Gypsy academics and mother-teachers: Gender, contingent labor, and Writing Program Administration*. Portsmouth, NH: Boynton/Cook-Heinemann.

Schemo, Diana. 2007. In war over teaching reading, a U.S.-local clash. *New York Times.*

Schoonmaker, Frances. 2002. *Growing up teaching: From personal knowledge to professional practice.* New York: Teachers' College Press.

Schuweis, Harold. 1995. Judaism: From either/or to both/and. In *Contemporary Jewish Ethics and Morality: A Reader,* ed. Elliot N. Dorff and Louis E. Newman, 25–37. New York: Oxford University Press.

Schuster, Charles. 1991. The politics of writing promotion. In *The Allyn and Bacon sourcebook for Writing Program Administrators,* ed. Irene Ward and William Carpenter, 331–41. New York: Longman.

———. 1995. Foreword. In *Resituating writing: Constructing and administering writing programs,* ed. Joseph Janangelo and Kristine Hansen, ix–xiv. Portsmouth, NH: Boynton/Cook-Heinemann.

Schwalm, David. 2002. The writing program (administrator) in context: Where am I, and can I still behave like a faculty member? In *The Allyn and Bacon sourcebook for writing program administrators,* ed. Irene Ward and William J. Carpenter, 9–22. New York: Longman.

Scott, Fred Newton. 1900. *Elementary English composition.* Boston: Allyn and Bacon.

———. 1926. *The standard of American speech.* Boston: Allyn and Bacon.

Scott, Tony. 2004. Managing labor and literacy in the future of composition studies. In *Tenured bosses and disposable teachers,* ed. Marc Bosquet, Tony Scott, and Leo Parascondola, 153–64. Carbondale: Southern Illinois University Press.

Sen, Rinku. 2003. *Stir it up: Lessons in community organizing and advocacy.* San Francisco: Jossey-Bass.

Shaughnessy, Mina. 1997. Diving in: An introduction to basic writing. In *Cross talk in composition,* ed. Victor Villanueva. Urbana, IL: NCTE, 1976.

Shenker-Osorio, Anat. 2006. Interview by Linda Adler-Kassner. September 15, 2006. San Francisco, CA.

Simpson, Susan. 2007. Study says freshman not ready: Colleges want high schools to provide more in-depth instruction across several subjects. *Daily Oklahoman,* April 10.

Skorczewski, Dawn M. 2005. *Teaching one moment at a time: Disruption and repair in the classroom.* Amherst: University of Massachusetts Press.

Slotkin, Richard. 1985. *The fatal environment: The myth of the frontier in the age of industrialization, 1800–1890.* New York: Atheneum.

Smith, Summer. 1997. The genre of the end comment: Conventions in teacher responses to student writing. *College Composition and Communication* 48 (2): 249–68.

Soliday, Mary. 2002. *The politics of remediation: Institutional and student needs in higher education.* Pittsburgh: University of Pittsburgh Press.

Solomon, Norman. 2006. Interview by Linda Adler-Kassner. September 17, 2006. Point Reyes Beach, CA.

Sommers, Nancy. 1982. Responding to student writing. *College Composition and Communication* 33 (2): 48–56.

Steinbacher, Michele. 2005. Clicking away at cheating. *Pantagraph,* April 10, 1.

Stephens, Scott. 2005. Double, double test is trouble: Even Shakespeare might struggle with SAT's new writing section. *Plain Dealer,* March 10, 1.

Straub, Richard. 1996. The concept of control in teacher response: Defining the varieties of directive and facilitative commentary. *College Composition and Communication* 47 (2): 223–51.

Straub, Richard, and Ronald Lunsford. 1995. *Twelve readers reading.* Creskill, NJ: Hampton Press.

Susman, Warren. 1984. *Culture as history.* New York: Pantheon.

Tallack, Douglas. 1991. *Twentieth century America: The intellectual and cultural context.* Longman Literature in English, ed. David Carroll and Michael Wheeler. London: Longman.

Taylor, Denny. 1998. *Beginning to read and the spin doctors of science: The political campaign to change America's mind about how children learn to read.* Urbana, IL: NCTE.

Telushkin, Rabbi Joseph. 1991. *Jewish literacy.* New York: William Morrow.

Thomasson, Dan K. 2005. Updated SATs still favor the best prepared students. *Ventura County Star,* March 11, 10.

Thompson, Frank. 1920. *The schooling of the immigrant.* New York and London: Harper and Brothers.

Thompson, Lynne. 2005. Educators blame Internet for rise in student cheating. *Seattle Times,* January 16, 1.

Thompson, Scott. 2005. *Leading from the eye of the storm: Spirituality and public school improvement.* Lanham, MD: Rowen and Littlefield Education.

Thorndike, Edward L. 1931. *Human Learning.* New York: The Century Company.

Tinto, Vincent. 1993. *Leaving college: Rethinking the causes and cures of student attrition.* 2nd ed., Chicago: University of Chicago Press.

Tobin, Lad. 2004. *Reading student writing: Confessions, meditations, and rants.* Portsmouth, NH: Boynton/Cook-Heinemann.

Tuchman, Gaye. 1978. *Making news: A study in the construction of reality.* New York: Free Press.

Tucker, Sarah Martinez. 2007. Opening Remarks. Regional Hearing on the Spellings Commission Report, Kansas City, MO.

Tyack, David. 2003. *Seeking common ground: Public schools in a diverse society.* Cambridge: Harvard University Press.

Vandenberg, Peter. 2007. Who is a writer?: What writers tell us. Produced by Linda Adler-Kassner and Dominic Delli Carpini and directed by Darsie Bowden. DVD.

Vander Lei, Elizabeth. 2005. Coming to terms with religious faith in the composition classroom. In *Negotiating religious faith,* ed. Elizabeth Vander Lei and Bonnie Kyburz, 3–10. Portsmouth, NH: Boynton/Cook.

———, and Bonnie Kyburz, ed. 2005. *Negotiating religious faith in the composition classroom.* Portsmouth, NH: Boynton/Cook.

Villanueva, Victor, ed. 1996. *Cross talk in comp theory.* Urbana, IL: NCTE.

_____. 2001. The Personal. In Symposium: The politics of the personal; Storying our lives against the grain. *College English* 64 (1): 50–52.

Volosinov, V. N. 1973. *Marxism and the philosophy of language,* trans. Ladislav Matejka and I.R.Titunik. Cambridge, MA: Harvard University Press.

Webb, Dean, Metha Arlene, and Forbis Jordan. 1996. *Foundations of American education.* Englewood Cliffs, NJ: Merrill.

Weisser, Christian. 2002. *Moving beyond academic discourse: Composition studies and the public sphere.* Carbondale: Southern Illinois University Press.

Wellstone Action. 2005. *Politics the Wellstone way: How to elect progressive candidates and win on issues.* Minneapolis: University of Minnesota Press.

West, Cornel. 1989. *The American evasion of philosophy: A geneology of pragmatism.* Madison: University of Wisconsin Press.

White, Hayden. 1978. *Tropics of discourse.* Baltimore: Johns Hopkins University Press.

Whiteclay, Chambers John. 1992. *The tyranny of change: America in the Progressive Era 1890–1920.* New York: St. Martin's.

Wiggins, Grant, and Jay McTighe. 1998. *Understanding by design.* Upper Saddle River, NJ: Prentice-Hall.

Will, George. 2007. Schools of choice growing. *Ann Arbor News*, February 1, 13.

Williams, Joseph. 2005. E-mail to Writing Program Administrators' Listserv. October 4, 2005.

Williamson, Kent. 2006. Telephone interview by Linda Adler-Kassner.

——. 2006. E-mail message to author, October 8.

Winerip, Michael. 2005. SAT essay test rewards length and ignores errors of fact. *New York Times*, May 4, 9.

Wise, Gene. 1973. *American historical explanations: A strategy for grounded inquiry.* Minneapolis: University of Minnesota Press

Woods, Mark. 2005. So how do you grade an SAT essay? *Florida Times-Union*, March 9, 1.

Writing Program Administrators (WPA), Council of. 1998. Evaluating the intellectual work of writing program administration. http://www.wpacouncil. org/positions/intellectualwork.html (accessed April 1, 2007).

——. 2000. WPA outcomes statement for first-year composition. http://www. wpacouncil.org/positions/outcomes.html (accessed March 10, 2007).

——. 2007. WPA position statement on assessment [draft]. http://www. wpacouncil.org/AssessmentPosition (accessed July 18, 2007).

Young, Morris. 2004. *Minor re/visions: Asian American literacy narratives as a rhetoric of citizenship.* Carbondale: Southern Illinois University Press.

Zoloth-Dorfman, Laurie. 1995. An ethics of encounter: Public choices and private acts. In *Contemporary Jewish ethics and morality: A reader*, ed. Elliot N. Dorff and Louis E. Newman, 219–245. New York: Oxford University Press.

INDEX

ABOUT THE AUTHOR

LINDA ADLER-KASSNER is Associate Professor of English and Director of First-Year Writing at Eastern Michigan University, where she teaches first-year writing and graduate courses in composition pedagogy and research. Thanks to the work of the fantastic EMU FYWP staff, their program was awarded a CCCC Writing Program Certificate of Excellence in 2005–2006. With Susanmarie Harrington, Linda is co-author of *Basic Writing as a Political Act: Public Stories about Writing and Literacy* and co-editor of *Questioning Authority: Stories Told in School*. With Greg Glau, she is co-editor of *The Bedford Bibliography for Teachers of Basic Writing*. Her research has also appeared in edited collections and journals, including *Journal of Basic Writing, College Composition and Communication, WPA Journal,* and *College English*. She is a former co-chair of the Conference on Basic Writing and currently Vice President of the Council of Writing Program Administrators.